To Garrett—my sun, my moon,
and all my stars

Contents

The Magic
of
Astrology

WHAT YOUR ZODIAC SIGN SAYS ABOUT
YOU (AND EVERYONE YOU KNOW)

JESSICA ALLEN

D

DRIVEN

Published in the United States by Driven, an imprint of Zeitgeist™, a division of Penguin Random House LLC, New York.
penguinrandomhouse.com

Produced by Girl Friday Productions

ISBN: 978-0-525-61729-7

Book design by Rachel Marek

Printed in the United States of America

3 5 7 9 10 8 6 4 2

Image credits (all credits belong to Shutterstock users): Cover, Mio Buono (stars & moons); Cover, Pixejoo (zodiac); 1-3, 21, Mio Buono (stars); 2-3, 8, 21-22, 34, 46, 58, 70, 82, 94, 106, 118, 130, 142, 154, Pixejoo (zodiac); 8, knstartstudio (sun); 10-11, Tamiris6 (constellations); 13, Daryaart9 (planets); 18, Pixejoo; 19, 166, Mio Buono; 22, 34, 46, 58, 70, 82, 94, 106, 118, 130, 142, 154, knstartstudio (chapter opener); 25, 37, 49, 61, 73, 85, 97, 121, 133, 145, 157, Daryaart9 (elements/planets); 25, 37, 49, 61, 73, 85, 97, 121, 133, 145, 157, Yeshe-la (swatch); 25, 37, 49, 61, 97, 109, Katya Zlobina (crystals/stones); 25, Vector Tradition (hawk); 25, Kaya Gach (flowers); 27, 39, 51, 63, 75, 87, 99, 111, 123, 135, 147, 159, Olha Yerofieieva; 29, Slastick_Anastasia Dudnyk (award); 29, 41, 137, 149, 174, Julia August (flags, sign, stop sign, game controller, sign, whistle); 31, Lutra_lutra (paint roller); 31, ArtCreationsDesignPhoto (passport); 33, FuzzyLogicKate (boxing gloves); 33, Loginova Li (rosemary); 37, 133 Tatyana Komtsyan (sloth, deer); 37, Mamsizz (lily); 41, Zamarashka (mixer); 43, Irina Vaneeva (plant); 43, Le Panda (Eiffel Tower); 45, 105, Daria Ustiugova (golf ball, skates); 45, 117, Gringoann (ylang-ylang, wisteria); 49, 145, Nikiparonak (butterfly, plant); 49, Angry_red_cat (snapdragon); 53, Fandorina Liza (origami); 53, khunchomvectors (calendar); 55, mimibubu (pillows); 55, 151, Inspiring (airplane, pagoda); 57, 69, Cat_arch_angel (tennis, goggles); 57, Galyna Gryshchenko (lilac); 61, 85, Anastasia Lembrik (dragonfly, bee); 61, arxichtu4ki (larkspur); 65, katu_water (scissors/thread); 65, 113, Galyna_P (heart, bubble); 67, anitapol (rug); 67, Elyaka (grapes); 69, Ekaterina Koroleva (basil); 73, 121, 145, Alena Solonshchikova (pyrite, turquoise, fluorite); 73, Angel Lina (ladybug); 73, Olga Korol (marigold); 77, Eisfrei; 79, 103, Atomorfen Illustration (chandelier, table); 79, Ollga P (bull); 81, 89, 125, 153, 161, Paulaparaula (soccer ball, whistle, foam finger, badminton, multipurpose tool); 81, Nataliya Ilnitska (cinnamon); 85, 133, 175, Myasnikova Natali (jade, amber, art supplies); 85, Katrine Glazkova (aster); 89, 101, 172, Maltiase (camera, headphones, scales, gavel); 91, Light Drop (flowers); 91, Dlinnychulok (boot); 93, Pikovit (bicycle); 93, Ortis (lily); 97, Naticka (flamingo); 97, Drvld (monstera); 103, 127, 139, hasiru (pyramids, Machu Picchu, Stonehenge); 105, anemad (geranium); 109, Lenny712 (wolf); 109, Natalia Zueva (peony); 113, aninata (popcorn); 115, le adhiz (wallpaper); 115, Maria Mirnaya (lantern); 117, S_O_Va (target); 121, Anna Pavlyuk (owl); 121, inoha (carnations); 125, KaterinaHol (thermometer); 127, AlexandraBonjour (horse); 129, Sharlotta (shoes); 129, Adelveys (iris); 133, Maria Goltsova (flower); 137, 173, DreamLoud (glue gun, book/magnifying glass); 139, 175, Mariia Kutuzova (teapot, vase); 141, Elena Biryukova (kayak); 141, Arefyeva Victoria (thyme); 145, Udod Lilia (otter); 151, atichat ammatayakul (lightbulb); 153, Gannie (flower); 157, Iya Balushkina (pearl); 157, MyStocks (dolphin); 157, Oleksandr Shatokhin (water lily); 161, flowerstock (sailboat); 163, Two over Two Studio (blue ombré); 163, 174, Rachel Moon (Space Needle, airplane); 165, Elinwool (water skis); 165, pansuang (hibiscus); 168, ridhobadal (heart); 169, Idrisalfath (lightning bolt); 172, RoseStudio (first aid kit); 172, Galina's Tales (frame); 173, AlexGreenArt (bus); 173, Plateresca (calculator); 174, Kamieshkova (newspaper); 175, Anastezia Luneva (blueprints)

Introduction

The Signs of Astrology

Right now, as you're reading these words, a baby is being born somewhere in the world. According to astrology, the precise position of the sun, the moon, the planets, and other astronomical bodies at this very moment can tell us about the kind of person that baby will become, their likes and dislikes, even what they might do for a living. It may seem like fortune-telling, but the magic of astrology is less about predicting the future than it is about having the power to see yourself clearly—and learn more about who you are.

Different cultures have different astrological systems, but each system shares the belief that we can glean remarkable knowledge about people from the locations of celestial objects at the time of their birth.

The zodiac of Western astrology has twelve signs. Although many factors have gone into making you the special person that you are, in astrology, the most important consideration is known as the zodiac sign, or sun sign. When someone asks, "What's your sign?" that's what they're talking about.

Each sign is named for a constellation through which the sun appears to move during a certain period of time during the year. Each has a corresponding element—fire, earth, air, or water—along with lucky days, preferred scents, special gems, symbolic animals, and much more. Signs with the same elements tend to have some similarities as well as the potential to be close friends.

Astrology Through the Ages

People have long relied on the night sky to navigate their lives. Our Stone Age ancestors notched the phases of the moon into bone some thirty-four thousand years ago, while sailors in the northern hemisphere have steered by the North Star for millennia.

Across eras and cultures, individuals began seeing patterns and shapes twinkling in the heavens above—what we call constellations—and they started telling stories about what they saw.

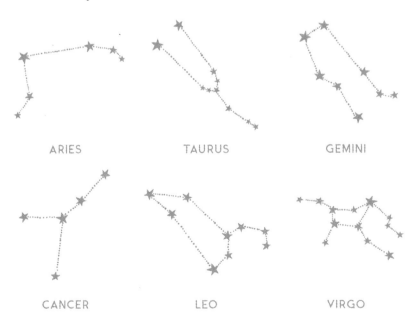

ARIES   TAURUS   GEMINI

CANCER   LEO   VIRGO

These interpretations took on predictive powers. By 1500 BCE, Babylonian priests in Mesopotamia had divided the sky into twelve parts. Each part of the zodiac was given a name, assigned certain symbols and colors, and ascribed different characteristics. Gods were connected to the sun, moon, and planets. After Alexander the Great conquered the area in 331 BCE, the Greeks took over the Babylonian astrological system, incorporating elements from Egypt.

For hundreds of years, astrology was inextricably bound to religion and politics. Roman rulers studied the horoscopes of their enemies and relied on astrologers to pinpoint auspicious dates for attacks. During the Renaissance, some Catholic popes consulted in-house astrologers, as did Queen Elizabeth. Shakespeare referenced astrology in his plays.

Astrology fell out of favor during the seventeenth and eighteenth centuries, known as the Age of Enlightenment.

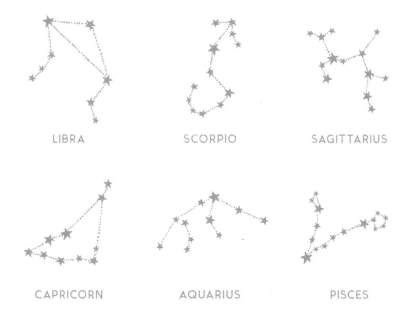

LIBRA   SCORPIO   SAGITTARIUS

CAPRICORN   AQUARIUS   PISCES

But, of course, astrology never died out. Instead, it broadened to encompass new planets, such as Uranus and Neptune, as they were discovered in the eighteenth and nineteenth centuries. By the 1960s, astrology had once again entered the mainstream, thanks to a generation of curious individuals looking to find answers about their place in the world.

Today, astrology is one of many tools we have to help us not only figure out but also appreciate what it means to be ourselves.

How the Planets Fit In

As with the sun in our solar system, our sun sign represents our core or very essence. It's the most powerful indicator of our personalities. Nevertheless, we're also affected by the planets and their relationship to one another.

The planets represent motivations, influences, and approaches. (In astrology, note that "planet" means "celestial body"—sometimes it's a moon, star, or minor planet.) As they move through the zodiac, they impact our lives.

Each sign is said to be ruled by at least one planet. Put another way: although every planet affects every sign, each planet has a special relationship with at least one sign. During that sign's time period, the planet will be at its strongest and most influential.

How the Houses Fit In

Along with the twelve signs of the zodiac, astrology has twelve houses, which oversee various parts of a person's life, such as money or friendship. Each house is ruled by a sign, and the house and its ruling sign share characteristics.

PLANET	SYMBOL	EFFECTS AND IMPACT	AFFILIATED ZODIAC SIGN
Sun	☉	Essence	Leo
Moon	☽	Emotions, instincts, nurturing	Cancer
Mercury	☿	Communication, intellect, thinking	Gemini and Virgo
Venus	♀	Beauty, love, pleasure	Libra and Taurus
Mars	♂	Action, aggression, energy	Aries and Scorpio
Jupiter	♃	Goals, luck, optimism	Pisces and Sagittarius
Saturn	♄	Boundaries, discipline	Aquarius and Capricorn
Uranus	♅	Innovation, originality	Aquarius
Neptune	♆	Dreams, insight, spirituality	Pisces
Pluto	♇	Growth, power, transformation	Scorpio

Your birth chart offers a map of everything at the moment of your birth, including the presence or absence of planets in the various houses. To get a birth chart, you'll need to know the exact time and location of your birth, although astrologers can make adjustments if you don't know specific details. (Plenty of sites online offer free birth charts, such as shop.astrology.com/birth-chart/.)

Having a planet in a particular house when you were born can bring out different facets of your sun sign, or determine areas of interest or importance to you. A house without

HOUSE	RULING SIGN	MAJOR CONCERNS
First	Aries	Appearance and personality, beginnings
Second	Taurus	Money
Third	Gemini	Communication
Fourth	Cancer	Family and home
Fifth	Leo	Creativity and fun
Sixth	Virgo	Health and well-being
Seventh	Libra	Relationships
Eighth	Scorpio	Transformations, including birth and death
Ninth	Sagittarius	Travel and adventure
Tenth	Capricorn	Career
Eleventh	Aquarius	Friendship and society
Twelfth	Pisces	Devotion and service, endings

a planet in it is still a part of your life, but it just might not be as relevant as a house with a planet. Some houses might have multiple planets in them. The more planets in a house, the more noteworthy that house.

In addition to the position of the planets, your birth chart will indicate your rising sign, or the sign that was on the cusp of the first house at the time of your birth. It's called the rising sign, or ascendant, because it was rising, or ascending, on the eastern horizon when you were born. Knowing your rising sign can give you clues about your character, especially if you've never felt totally in sync with your sun sign. Since it's affiliated with the first house, your rising sign is associated with your personality and how people perceive you.

Astrology and You

Astrology can help you develop your strengths and face your personal challenges. It's a tool for looking inward and figuring out who you are—and how you can grow as a person. It's a way to reflect on your relationships and find inspiration for your future. It truly is magical.

In addition to helping you uncover facets of your personality, astrology can help you better comprehend your body. Each sign is associated with an organ, biological system, body part, or muscle group. Considering the connections between signs and areas of the body creates a more nuanced awareness of astrology's physical and psychological components throughout our lives.

Please remember to always get regular checkups and to consult with a medical professional in the event of any worries or questions.

The Zodiac Body

SIGN	ASSOCIATED PARTS OF THE BODY
Aries	Face, head
Taurus	Neck, throat, vocal cords
Gemini	Arms, hands, lungs, respiratory system
Cancer	Chest, heart
Leo	Spine, upper back
Virgo	Digestive system
Libra	Kidneys, lower back
Scorpio	Reproductive system, sexual organs
Sagittarius	Hips, liver, thighs
Capricorn	Bones, joints, teeth
Aquarius	Ankles, circulatory system
Pisces	Feet, immune system, lymphatic system

Zodiac Signs Quick Guide

Every sign is multifaceted and profound, as you'll see in the chapters to come. But here's a quick guide to decoding all twelve.

SIGN	DATES	ELEMENT	WHAT DEFINES THIS SIGN?	WHAT COULD THIS SIGN USE MORE OF?
Aries	Mar 21–Apr 19	Fire	They act	Patience
Taurus	Apr 20–May 20	Earth	They acquire	Change
Gemini	May 21–Jun 20	Air	They chatter	Calmness
Cancer	Jun 21–Jul 22	Water	They care	Confidence
Leo	Jul 23–Aug 22	Fire	They perform	Humility
Virgo	Aug 23–Sep 22	Earth	They serve	Downtime
Libra	Sep 23–Oct 22	Air	They balance	Decisiveness
Scorpio	Oct 23–Nov 21	Water	They want	Openheartedness
Sagittarius	Nov 22–Dec 21	Fire	They roam	Tact
Capricorn	Dec 22–Jan 19	Earth	They strive	Fun
Aquarius	Jan 20–Feb 18	Air	They invent	Emotion
Pisces	Feb 19–Mar 20	Water	They feel	Boundaries

The Zodiac Wheel

Every aspect of the zodiac wheel reveals a vital element of each sun sign.

THE SIGN'S
SYMBOL

THE SIGN'S
PRIMARY ELEMENT

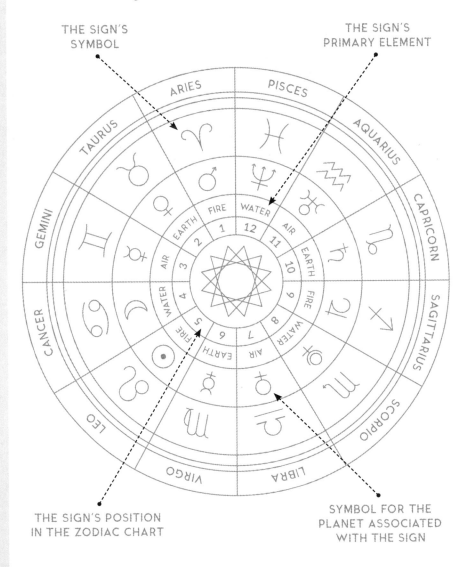

THE SIGN'S POSITION
IN THE ZODIAC CHART

SYMBOL FOR THE
PLANET ASSOCIATED
WITH THE SIGN

How To Use This Book

To get a sense of the complete zodiac, you might wish to begin with Aries and read this book straight through. But you definitely don't have to go through this book in any special order. You can flip straight to your zodiac sign, or turn to a certain section to learn more about someone in your life. Each chapter covers various aspects of the signs, from health and well-being to friends and family to places you should visit, with an emphasis on each sign's most notable traits.

Astrology offers valuable insight into our personalities and preferences. However, as complex creatures, we contain an array of characteristics, and we are affected by our unique experiences. Not every description of your sign might fit or speak to you. That's OK! You can still use this book to deepen your understanding of yourself and those around you by thinking of different traits as tendencies or likelihoods, rather than as absolutes. We all have the ability to choose how we interact with the world. Nothing is set in stone.

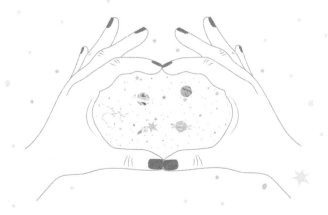

What If You're on the Cusp?

If your birthday falls in the two to three days before one sign ends and after another begins, you're considered to be on the cusp of two signs. The best way to figure out your true zodiac sign is to get a birth chart done. In reality, you might feel as if you have elements of both signs, so it could benefit you to learn about the two signs you straddle.

Dates on the Cusp:

Aries-Taurus: 4/16–4/22

Taurus-Gemini: 5/17–5/23

Gemini-Cancer: 6/17–6/23

Cancer-Leo: 7/19–7/25

Leo-Virgo: 8/19–8/25

Virgo-Libra: 9/19–9/25

Libra-Scorpio: 10/19–10/25

Scorpio-Sagittarius: 11/18–11/24

Sagittarius-Capricorn: 12/18–12/24

Capricorn-Aquarius: 1/16–1/22

Aquarius-Pisces: 2/15–2/21

Pisces-Aries: 3/17–3/23

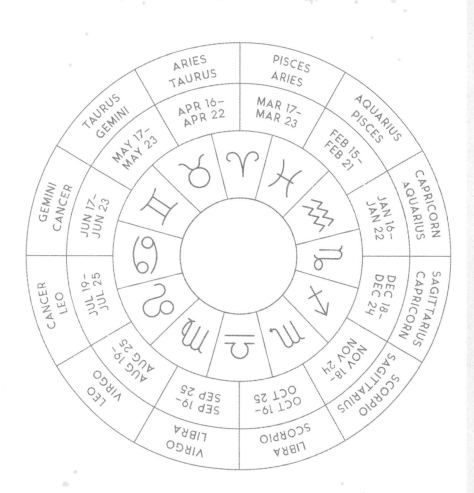

Aries

THE RAM

March 21 – April 19

All About Aries

People born under Aries are natural leaders and independent thinkers, with a go-getting approach to pretty much everything. Such dynamism means they do not tolerate those who would stand in their way. After all, this sign is connected to Mars, the Roman god of war, and is symbolized by the ram. Butting heads is no big deal for Aries.

Being so gutsy requires confidence and bravery, and Aries have plenty of both, along with the courage of their convictions. They have no trouble standing up for (and, if necessary, fighting for) what they believe. As the first sign of the zodiac, Aries folks love fresh beginnings, blazing trails, and coming out on top. Indeed, this sign is among the most competitive, and the most brash. That combination means Aries can sometimes come across as having a "me first" attitude.

Passionate, outgoing, and energetic, Aries relishes action. Predictability, stability, and routine—not so much. Follow-through can sometimes be a problem, but Aries is brimming with self-confidence and vision. As a result, Aries inspires and motivates loads of people in all kinds of situations. A team with Aries at the helm is virtually unstoppable.

Things Aries Is Really Good At

Aries folks are all about action—they set goals, take charge, and appreciate challenges. They do not shy away from a fight, which makes them fierce defenders, committed activists, and strong leaders.

Ways Aries Can Stretch Themselves

Pausing to reflect and evaluate is hard for a doer like Aries. But sometimes taking a step back shows the best way forward.

Strengths and Weaknesses

STRENGTHS	WEAKNESSES
☐ Animated	☐ Aggressive
☐ Brave	☐ Argumentative
☐ Confident	☐ Fearful
☐ Courageous	☐ Impatient
☐ Dynamic	☐ Impulsive
☐ Frank	☐ Opinionated
☐ Passionate	☐ Quick-tempered

ELEMENT

Fire

RULED BY

Mars

COLORS

Eggplant, red, rust

GEMS AND MINERALS

Amethyst, diamond, garnet

ANIMALS AND INSECTS

Fire ant, hawk,
ram, wildcat

PLANTS AND FLOWERS

Calendula, impatiens,
zebra plant

FAMOUS ARIES

Lady Gaga, Yayoi Kusama,
Lil Nas X, Colin Powell, Paul Rudd,
Kristen Stewart, Vincent van Gogh,
Reese Witherspoon

Friendship and Family

Although they are independent and self-confident, those with Aries as their sign nonetheless display a lot of devotion to loved ones. Friends admire Aries' motivation, inner strength, and daring. Full of fire, Aries never make for dull company.

Like the ram, their zodiac animal, Aries can have hard heads. They are honest and frank, almost to a fault, which sometimes alienates those who prefer a more tactful demeanor. Others love the Aries lack of pretension and willingness to tell it like it is.

Aries trust themselves and have a lot of faith in their opinions. This attitude can cause problems when it comes time to compromise or accept someone else's authority. But everyone, including quick-tempered Aries, has to take orders once in a while. For traditionally headstrong Aries, it's worth remembering that following someone else's advice isn't a sign of weakness.

How to Get Along with Aries

- ☐ Enjoy having adventures (don't be boring!)
- ☐ Give space and encourage Aries independence
- ☐ Respond quickly to messages (don't make Aries wait!)

Signs Aries Gets Along With

Aquarius
Gemini
Leo
Sagittarius

Signs Who Don't Always Get Aries

Cancer
Capricorn
Libra

Out and About

Full of hustle, Aries likes to go and to do. Aries starts the day running (sometimes literally), with a sense of drive and purpose, and stays up to date on the hottest trends.

Aries prefers to tackle tiny portions of several projects at once. This sign thrives on speed, high pressure, and a fast pace—don't expect Aries to stay in one place or on one task for long.

Aries enjoys meeting friends for lunch, particularly if the restaurant recently opened and is getting good buzz, and they won't hesitate to pick up the check. With a love of the new, Aries folks would rather discuss current events than reminisce about old times. And, with an opinion on everything, Aries tends to offer advice, regardless of whether it's requested.

Woe to the person holding up the line at the grocery store or exiting too slowly off the highway. This sign expects everyone, and everything, to exhibit the same level of Aries certainty and intensity, or at least stay out of their way.

Lucky Day	Lucky Number
Tuesday	9

Activities Aries Enjoys

- ☐ Capoeira
- ☐ Car and bike racing
- ☐ Drumming
- ☐ Extreme sports like motocross, hot yoga, skydiving

Things That Challenge Aries

- ☐ Ambiguity
- ☐ Being ignored
- ☐ Coming in second
- ☐ Meditation and mindfulness
- ☐ Vagueness
- ☐ Wasting time

Home and Away

Prone to restlessness, Aries don't have an innate nesting instinct. At home, Aries like to be as busy as they are everywhere else. You're more likely to find Aries redecorating the bedroom or rearranging some bookshelves than simply hanging out. For this reason, Aries homes tend to be always changing—and usually clean.

Their intrepid, enthusiastic personalities make Aries folks excellent travel companions, as long as you don't want to linger in any one spot for too long. They take delays, lost luggage, and other nuisances in stride, and don't mind traveling without a firm plan. What matters most to Aries is heading out and having an adventure.

In line with their love of risk-taking and their obsession with the new, Aries enjoys exploring and going where few have gone before. A guided tour, in which they're meant to passively absorb facts about a place, will put them straight to sleep, unless the tour is coupled with something adventurous or physical like biking or hiking.

Where Is Aries Most at Home?

This fire sign thrives in hot, arid climates, such as the desert. Backcountry camping or traveling to remote destinations appeals to their pioneering personality.

Ways to Design Your Space to Align with Aries

☐ Embrace bold colors—the overall vibe
  should be dramatic or even audacious
☐ Mix patterns
☐ Light a fire or burn candles
  to convey Aries passion

Places Aries Definitely Needs to Travel To

☐ Alice Springs and Uluru, Australia
☐ Buenos Aires, Argentina
☐ Cappadocia, Turkey
☐ Florence, Italy
☐ Grand Canyon, Arizona, United States
☐ Nashville, Tennessee, United States
☐ Skeleton Coast National Park, Namibia

Health and Wellness

Intense exercise fuels Aries, giving this sign even more energy. All the better if the exercise has an element of danger or risk—mountain biking or rock climbing, for example. Aries has lots of natural adrenaline and doesn't seem to need as much sleep as other signs—though Aries should remember that being well rested will help them make smart choices during their adventures.

The constant drive to do and act leads to stress and tension. It can also lead to burnout. Taking time to relax and rejuvenate is fundamental, if difficult for Aries to do.

Facials, head massages, and acupuncture can force Aries to slow down for a spell, and even relieve some of the headaches, migraines, and sinus infections to which they're prone.

Things That Nourish Aries

Aries particularly enjoys spicy food and bold flavors. An Aries will almost never say no to meat, but vegetarian Aries can compromise with hearty dishes like grilled Halloumi or portobello mushrooms. Visiting a sauna or taking a hot bath helps stimulate the natural Aries passion for life, while a head massage can help cool the sizzling Aries brain.

Favorite Ways to Be Active

Boxing, downhill skiing, judo,
mixed martial arts (MMA), mountain
biking, rock climbing, running

Ailments and Injuries to Watch Out For

Aggression, eye strain,
headaches and migraines, jaw pain,
panic attacks, sinus infections

Scents and Essential Oils

Bergamot, clove, frankincense,
kunzea, neroli, rosemary

Taurus

THE BULL

April 20 – May 20

All About Taurus

Taurus understands the art of living. This sign values beauty and pleasure—from a rich, creamy dessert to a hip-shaking song to a velvety weighted blanket. "Life is good" could be the Taurus motto.

Yet Taurus knows that a good life takes hard work. Tauruses are industrious, determined, and committed. Once Taurus makes a plan or decides on a course of action, there's no further discussion or deviation. While this laser-like focus aids Taurus in achieving goals, it also makes for some serious stubbornness. Taurus dislikes change.

You won't see Taurus chasing the latest trends or contorting themselves to fit in. Instead, Tauruses feel comfortable and confident in their own skin. Their self-assuredness is naturally magnetic, balanced by a practical, earthy side.

Tauruses love their stuff, preferring possessions to experiences. They have an expert eye for quality. Being surrounded by their own gorgeous things is the Taurus happy place; it helps them feel secure. Along with this desire to accumulate, however, comes a difficulty with letting go. Unfortunately, that can include grudges. Learning to forgive and forget might take Taurus a lifetime to master.

Things Taurus Is Really Good At

Taurus has excellent taste and a discriminating appreciation for beauty. Trust Taurus recommendations for art, fashion, food, music, and deluxe self-care. This sign also has a knack for making and saving money.

Ways Tauruses Can Stretch Themselves

Taurus needs to learn to let go. For this sign, security comes from possessing. More is always more. Taurus has trouble recognizing when it's time to say goodbye—to an object they no longer love or a plan that no longer makes sense.

Strengths and Weaknesses

STRENGTHS	WEAKNESSES
☐ Dependable	☐ Acquisitive
☐ Determined	☐ Decadent
☐ Down to earth	☐ Inflexible
☐ Kind	☐ Insecure
☐ Reliable	☐ Resentful
☐ Stable	☐ Stubborn
☐ Warm	☐ Unbending

ELEMENT

Earth

RULED BY

Venus

COLORS

Green, light pink

GEMS AND MINERALS

Emerald, malachite, rose quartz

ANIMALS AND INSECTS

Bear, bull, dog, sloth

PLANTS AND FLOWERS

Heartleaf philodendron, lily, thyme

FAMOUS TAURUSES

Jessica Alba, David Beckham, Dwayne Johnson, Lizzo, Jerry Seinfeld, William Shakespeare, Barbra Streisand, Kenan Thompson

Friendship and Family

Feeling down? Seek out Taurus. These affectionate friends stand ready with a kind word or bear hug, and they will never let you down. Even-keeled and stable, with a lovely, calm disposition, they make for terrific couch companions for binge-watching. But be prepared to clean up, as Taurus will likely be too comfy to do it.

Big hugs and a love of cuddles notwithstanding, Taurus isn't a pushover. With friends and family, Taurus can be willful, especially when someone else's notions conflict with their intended plans. Tantrums in Taurus children can grow into angry spells in Taurus adults. If pushed or prodded too hard, Taurus—like its bull symbol—may very well charge right back.

How to Get Along with Taurus

☐ Be a homebody
☐ Follow the plan (go with the Taurus flow)
☐ Give nice presents
☐ Offer to clean up

Signs Taurus Gets Along With

Cancer
Capricorn
Pisces
Virgo

Signs Who Don't Always Get Taurus

Aquarius
Leo
Scorpio

Out and About

Sleeping in doesn't usually work for Taurus, despite this sign's reputation for being slow to get started. After a sweat session, which will probably be (1) a blend of cardio and strength training, and (2) a beloved, long-established routine, Taurus opts for a luxurious bath. There will be bath bombs, loads of essential oils, and maybe a mask or three.

A true Taurus has no problem spending the day at home, puttering, organizing, and admiring their exquisite possessions. Expect some straight-up lounging as well. Taurus completes work and other tasks slowly, steadily, and diligently, with plenty of time set aside for self-care. Why rush?

Tauruses like to shop, specifically at high-end brick-and-mortar stores, where they can get a feel for the goods before they buy. You'll also find Taurus exploring art museums, attending concerts, and generally deepening the sign's well-known interest in culture. At the end of the day, Tauruses enjoy sharing what they saw and heard over a decadent multicourse meal.

Lucky Day	Lucky Number
Friday	10

Activities Taurus Enjoys

- ☐ Collecting art
- ☐ Cooking and baking
- ☐ Making jewelry
- ☐ Playing music and singing
- ☐ Shopping
- ☐ Spa time and self-care routines

Things That Challenge Taurus

- ☐ Austerity
- ☐ Change
- ☐ Compromise
- ☐ Denial
- ☐ Fickleness
- ☐ Moving too fast
- ☐ Not having ˚enough˚

Home and Away

For some signs, "homebody" might be an insult. Not so with Taurus, who loves to nest and feels safest and most secure when surrounded by material things. A Taurean home is a cozy, peaceful place to be, with candles, blankets, art books, and plush furniture begging to be lazed upon.

Taurus tends to accumulate and could benefit from periodic downsizing or decluttering, painful as it might be for Taurus to part with anything. With their love of at-home spa treatments and skin-care routines, their bathrooms, in particular, could likely use a little pruning.

When traveling, Tauruses prefer to take their time, whether that's exploring a famed museum or going for a walk in the woods. A planner by nature, Taurus happily follows an itinerary and delights in organized events. In terms of where to go, luxury and comfort are key considerations.

Where Is Taurus Most at Home?

Where Taurus goes is perhaps less significant than where they get to stay—and what kind of amenities they'll find when they get there. Taurus likes the outdoors, but enjoys nature even more while glamping or from the vantage point of a luxury spa.

Ways to Design Your Space
to Align with Taurus

- ☐ Offset cream-colored walls
  with earth-toned accents
- ☐ Incorporate lots of textures, in keeping
  with the Taurean love of touch
- ☐ Display beloved collections or objets d'art
- ☐ Grow an indoor herb garden

Places Taurus Definitely
Needs to Travel To

- ☐ Banff, Canada
- ☐ Cape Town, South Africa
- ☐ Goa, India
- ☐ Paris, France
- ☐ San Juan, Puerto Rico
- ☐ Sonoma, California, United States
- ☐ Tuscany, Italy

Health and Wellness

Good health for this persevering sign means not only setting goals but hammering away until the goals are met, whether that's perfecting a new sport or doing a record number of squats. Tauruses tend to be strong.

As carnal creatures, Tauruses adore gooey, delicious dishes. Taurus will eat all the pasta *and* all the tiramisu. Occasionally indulging such cravings is fine. However, over-indulging, as Taurus is wont to do, can lead to a sense of sluggishness. To feel their best, Tauruses might focus on practicing moderation and mindfulness. ˉ

To combat any tendency toward slothfulness and prevent Taurus from falling into a rut, this sign should opt for high-energy, fun playlists when working out. They like high-end gear, too.

Things That Nourish Taurus

For Taurus, the world's extraordinary beauty is a kind of luxury. A hike, scored with nature's chorus or real music, fills the Taurus soul, and a post-hike smoothie with lots of tropical fruit provides the healthy indulgence they crave.

Favorite Ways to Be Active

Boot-camp workouts, cycling, geocaching, golf, lifting weights, and bodybuilding

Ailments and Injuries to Watch Out For

Colds, earaches, insecurity, laryngitis, resentment, thyroid disorders

Scents and Essential Oils

Amber, honeysuckle, magnolia, patchouli, vanilla, ylang-ylang

Gemini

THE TWINS

May 21 – June 20

All About Gemini

The third sign in the Zodiac, Gemini is symbolized by the Twins. But rather than being two-faced or duplicitous, Gemini is the ultimate multitasker, capable of being—and doing—many things at once. People born under this sign have countless interests, friends, and thoughts they love to share. Prepare to be charmed.

It's no surprise that bubbly Gemini's animals and insects include birds and butterflies. This social sign loves floating from gathering to gathering and group to group, and brings positive, outgoing energy wherever it lands. Along with being first-rate networkers, Geminis are excellent communicators. They're charismatic, articulate, and friendly, prone to gesturing with their hands as they enthuse about their latest passion. Blessed with the gift of gab, Geminis will never turn down the chance to talk it out.

Geminis have bright minds and seemingly limitless curiosity. Despite their reputation for nonstop sociability and chatter, they're quite intellectual and delight in the exchange of ideas. Like a sparrow feathering its nest, Gemini gathers and stores information. They gravitate toward the new, with little patience for routine, rigor, or anything remotely boring.

Things Gemini Is Really Good At

Gemini soaks up facts, which makes this sign a quick learner. An outgoing nature helps Gemini excel at team projects or sports that require collaboration, since people are drawn to Gemini insights and appreciate this sign's adaptability.

Ways Geminis Can Stretch Themselves

Being endlessly curious means Gemini has a million different interests. But it also means Gemini is prone to zooming from passion to passion. Choosing one or two to really focus on—and cultivating a stick-to-it mindset—will help curb any tendency toward flightiness.

Strengths and Weaknesses

STRENGTHS	WEAKNESSES
☐ Adaptable	☐ Easily overwhelmed
☐ Clever	☐ Exaggerating
☐ Connected	☐ Lacking discipline
☐ Curious	☐ Quickly bored
☐ Easygoing	☐ Rash
☐ Knowledgeable	☐ Self-conscious
☐ Outgoing	☐ Superficial

ELEMENT

Air

RULED BY

Mercury

COLORS

Light green, yellow

GEMS AND MINERALS

Agate, citrine,
tiger's-eye

ANIMALS AND INSECTS

Butterfly, mockingbird,
monkey, sparrow

PLANTS AND FLOWERS

Iris, mint, snapdragon

FAMOUS GEMINIS

Awkwafina, Peter Dinklage,
Bob Dylan, Naomi Campbell,
Lucy Hale, Kendrick Lamar,
Marilyn Monroe, Prince

Friendship and Family

When it comes to friends, Gemini is bighearted and benevolent, enthusiastic and energetic. This sign is also flirty and fun, the life of every party. As a super-social creature, Gemini tends to have a big group of friends. While Gemini gravitates toward people who can match the fabled Gemini wit and keep up their side of the conversation, those born under this sign can talk to and become friends with just about anyone.

Gemini has a lot of patience for younger siblings or relatives. Kids respond to Gemini's effervescence and stockpile of random fun facts. Everyone loves the Gemini sense of humor. Communication matters a lot to Geminis, and they are especially good at defusing tension when conversation tips into heated discussions or arguments.

With a quick, versatile mind, Gemini is always mentally on the move. But Gemini could benefit from slowing down and sincerely listening to friends and family. They should beware of gossiping, too—it's better to say nothing than to say something potentially unkind or untrue.

How to Get Along with Gemini

☐ Ask questions
☐ Be an entertaining conversationalist
☐ Embrace adventure
☐ Have a good sense of humor

Signs Gemini Gets Along With

Aquarius
Aries
Leo
Libra

Signs Who Don't Always Get Gemini

Pisces
Sagittarius
Virgo

Out and About

Warning: Just hearing about a Gemini day may make non-Geminis feel exhausted. Indeed, so humongous is the Gemini fear of boredom that this sign may double-book, in addition to scheduling multiple back-to-back activities. Honestly, there's no such thing as a typical Gemini day, since this sign dislikes routine, preferring spontaneity and novelty.

On the rare occasion Geminis lack plans, they go out and find something fun to do and someone fun to do it with. For Geminis, a stranger is a friend they haven't met yet. And then it's on to the next thing, and the next, and the next. This nonstop activity can prevent Gemini from living in, and truly enjoying, the moment—or the person sharing it.

As part of this sociability, Gemini loves to share and communicate. From the time they wake up until the time they go to sleep, Geminis are talking, texting, writing, posting, calling, blogging, podcasting . . . you name it.

Lucky Day	Lucky Number
Wednesday	11

Activities Gemini Enjoys

- ☐ Joining a book club
- ☐ Learning a new language
- ☐ Origami
- ☐ Socializing
- ☐ Team sports
- ☐ Writing

Things That Challenge Gemini

- ☐ Boredom
- ☐ Lack of plans
- ☐ Loneliness
- ☐ Repetition and routine
- ☐ Sameness
- ☐ Silence

Home and Away

The Gemini love of socializing makes this sign an ideal guest and enviable host, known for their excellent soirees. As such, Gemini needs space to entertain, from little nooks for intimate conversations to larger areas for dinner or dance parties.

In addition to zones for entertaining, Gemini must have various places to store the array of books, magazines, and other media this sign acquires due to their insatiable curiosity. When it comes to Gemini, school is always in session; this sign never stops hungering for knowledge.

Travel is one of the many ways Gemini learns. Always up for an adventure, Gemini makes for a spirited travel partner. As social creatures, they relish the opportunity to chat with people wherever they go. Cities not only give this sign the experiences they crave but also encourage Gemini to form tons of brand-new connections and discover new things.

Where Is Gemini Most at Home?

For Gemini, nothing beats the sights, sounds, smells, and vitality of the city. There are new friends and adventures around every corner.

Ways to Design Your Space to Align with Gemini

- ☐ Offer a variety of seating options, from big pillows on the floor to comfy chairs
- ☐ Choose bright colors to match the bright Gemini personality
- ☐ Pick pairs where possible (two chairs, two mirrors, two even stacks of books, and so on)
- ☐ Keep supplies on hand for easy entertaining

Places Gemini Definitely Needs to Travel To

- ☐ Berlin, Germany
- ☐ Dubai, United Arab Emirates
- ☐ Hong Kong
- ☐ Istanbul, Turkey
- ☐ Las Vegas, Nevada, United States
- ☐ Rio de Janeiro, Brazil
- ☐ Tokyo, Japan

Health and Wellness

Routine bores Gemini, so one way this sign stays healthy is to keep exercise fresh, both in general and during specific sessions. At the gym, Geminis should sign up for different HIIT or dance classes. When possible, Geminis like to talk as they move. Team sports let them simultaneously socialize and work out.

But Gemini also likes to move the mind as well as the body. One-on-one sports that require a nice dose of strategy, like tennis or racquetball, satisfy the Gemini desire for brainwork.

Gemini is associated with the nervous system as well as the hands, lungs, shoulders, and arms. Talking with their hands can sometimes throw the Gemini neck out of whack. Gemini needs to take care when they get excited (which is often) so that they don't overdo the gestures.

Other signs envy the youthful Gemini glow, the result of a lively spirit and go-with-the-flow attitude. Having snacks on hand will ensure that Gemini energy never flags.

Things That Nourish Gemini

The consummate juggler, Gemini does best when doing many things at once—hanging out with friends, telling stories, having adventures, learning new things. It's the constant motion, more than the activity itself, that replenishes Gemini energy.

Favorite Ways to Be Active

High-intensity interval training (HIIT),
hip-hop, hockey, modern dance,
tennis, rowing, volleyball

Ailments and Injuries to Watch Out For

Asthma, coughs, feeling overwhelmed,
insomnia, restlessness, stiff neck

Scents and Essential Oils

Lavender, lemongrass, lilac,
peppermint, sweet pea

Cancer

THE CRAB

June 21–July 22

All About Cancer

Cancer is represented by the crab, but it could just as easily have been symbolized by a fennec fox (with big ears for listening) or an octopus (with lots of arms for holding someone close). Even a snail could work, since it carries around its home—Cancer's favorite place. Cancers adore being at home.

This sign loves to nurture, protect, and care for others. In fact, some astrologers refer to Cancer as the zodiac "mom."

Still, a crab's a crab. Cancer can be difficult to pin down, scuttling around an issue rather than confronting it head-on. They can also be a bit hardheaded, singularly focused on achieving a goal. Moody and mercurial, they seek to avoid conflict. But beneath their tough exterior is a soft, vulnerable creature, almost eerily empathetic and attuned to feelings. So many feelings.

With this deep sensitivity comes a tendency to be wounded. One wrong word or whiff of danger sends Cancers right back into their shells, pinching as they go. Sometimes this danger is real, and sometimes it's imagined. This touchy sign has a habit of seeing catastrophes everywhere. Nonetheless, you'll have trouble finding a better friend.

Things Cancer Is Really Good At

Mentoring comes naturally to Cancer, as this sign takes pride in the success of others. So does unconditional listening (no judgments here!). Creative Cancers excel at making and crafting, weaving their love of others into their art.

Ways Cancers Can Stretch Themselves

Cancers sometimes have trouble revealing vulnerability. Trying to put their own needs first or asking for help causes a lot of inner turmoil. Scary as it is, letting people in is fundamental.

Strengths and Weaknesses

STRENGTHS	WEAKNESSES
☐ Considerate	☐ Delicate
☐ Creative	☐ Indirect
☐ Empathetic	☐ Moody
☐ Intuitive	☐ Narrow-minded
☐ Loving	☐ Overly emotional
☐ Loyal	☐ Timid
☐ Protective	☐ Unpredictable

ELEMENT
Water

RULED BY
The Moon

COLORS
Indigo, silver, white

GEMS AND MINERALS
Moonstone,
ocean jasper, ruby

ANIMALS AND INSECTS
Crab, dragonfly,
sea lion, turtle

PLANTS AND FLOWERS
Aloe, bamboo, larkspur

FAMOUS CANCERS
Kristen Bell, Gisele Bündchen,
Ariana Grande, Tom Hanks,
Frida Kahlo, Thurgood Marshall,
Elon Musk, Meryl Streep

Friendship and Family

Among the most family-oriented creatures of the zodiac signs, Cancer really and truly cares. This sign puts family—whether biological or chosen—first. Doing so makes for incredibly strong bonds. Cancer is the supreme cheerleader, nurturer, protector, and supporter. Consider yourself lucky if you have one in your corner.

Yet, this care can come at a cost. Cancers sometimes neglect their own needs, and they are prone to swallowing a slight until it grows into a wound, then retreating into defensiveness. Even more dangerous, this sign can fall prey to those who might seek to take advantage of their unselfish and doting ways. A hard shell is one thing, but Cancers need to have a backbone, too.

Sentimental, intuitive, and creative, Cancers give thoughtful presents, like homemade cards, cakes, or crafts, for any and every occasion.

How to Get Along with Cancer

☐ Be appreciative of Cancer's generosity
☐ Fit in quality time
☐ Share your feelings
☐ Speak and act with kindness

Signs Cancer Gets Along With

Pisces
Scorpio
Taurus
Virgo

Signs Who Don't Always Get Cancer

Aries
Capricorn
Libra

Out and About

Cancer is largely content to stay at, or very close to, home. The joys of the outside world pale in comparison to the comfort of a Cancer abode, particularly when friends and family arrive to play games, share a meal, or just hang out. Cancer revels in reminiscing as much as in making new memories.

That said, Cancer isn't a recluse, and especially enjoys being out and about in nature. As a water sign, Cancer gravitates toward anything aquatic, be it an ocean, lake, creek, or river. Like the water, Cancers have ups and downs. Frolicking in or near water helps Cancer stay steady.

Wherever they go, Cancers prefer the known over the unknown. Familiarity is another way to help ease this sign out of its shell. As a result, Cancers can get as attached to places as to people.

Lucky Day	Lucky Number
Monday	2

Activities Cancer Enjoys

- ☐ Being in or near water
- ☐ Crafting
- ☐ Cuddling
- ☐ Hanging out at home
- ☐ Journaling
- ☐ Scrapbooking
- ☐ Sewing
- ☐ Taking care of people and pets

Things That Challenge Cancer

- ☐ Asking for help
- ☐ Breakups
- ☐ Discord
- ☐ Rejection
- ☐ Powerlessness
- ☐ Secrets
- ☐ Taking risks

Home and Away

Home matters to Cancer. It's where Cancer feels safest and most grounded; it's where this sign can let go of the needs of others and concentrate on their own for once (or try to). For Cancer, home is the ultimate retreat.

Curtains and dividing walls are some of the ways Cancers fashion a secluded hideaway from the world. But this sentimental sign can't stand to be away from friends and family for long. Cancers enjoy entertaining and frequently have folks over. In addition, the Cancer home will overflow with photos and mementos that tap into Cancer's nostalgic side. Occasionally getting rid of the excess ensures that truly special reminders receive pride of place.

It's not that Cancer doesn't like to travel. Rather, Cancer prefers a trip that lets them establish a comfortable home base close to any loved ones who live nearby. This sign favors the familiar over the new, so Cancer will usually find a favorite vacation spot, ideally by the water, to return to year after year.

Where Is Cancer Most at Home?

Anywhere near water will gladden the Cancer heart. Beaches are good, but islands are even better. So is a space big enough to hold cherished friends, family, and pets.

Ways to Design Your Space to Align with Cancer

- ☐ Harmonize—everything should blend and match
- ☐ Keep the flow as open as possible
- ☐ Add area rugs for coziness
- ☐ Utilize open shelving to display interesting items

Places Cancer Definitely Needs to Travel To

- ☐ Crete, Greece
- ☐ Finger Lakes, New York, United States
- ☐ Galápagos Islands, Ecuador
- ☐ Kauai, Hawaii, United States
- ☐ Madagascar
- ☐ Maldives
- ☐ Martha's Vineyard, Massachusetts, United States
- ☐ Turks and Caicos

Health and Wellness

Food plays a starring role in Cancer's life. This sign often shows affection by whipping up big, delicious meals for friends and family. Cancer takes tremendous pleasure in the rituals of dining, from baking or cooking with loved ones to having conversations at the table.

The flip side of being such a devoted foodie is a sensitive stomach. When Cancer worries—which, frankly, is kind of a lot—the anxieties seem to center right in the core. Some Cancers eat too much in an attempt to calm the fears; others don't eat enough. Figuring out healthy ways to deal with stress should be a Cancer priority.

Cancer also needs to concentrate on self-care. Putting others first sustains Cancer, for sure. But spending time alone—whether reading, journaling, doing yoga, or playing with a pet—fuels this sign's introspection and heightens its intuition.

Things That Nourish Cancer

Nurturing others nourishes Cancer. This sign lives to listen, hug, help, care for, make things for, and feed everyone they love, both two-legged and four-legged.

Favorite Ways to Be Active

Beach running, hatha or vinyasa yoga,
Pilates, stretch-and-tone workouts,
swimming, water aerobics

Ailments and Injuries to Watch Out For

Acid reflux, fear of crowds,
heartburn, hypersensitivity,
possessiveness, upset stomach

Scents and Essential Oils

Balsam of Peru, basil, chamomile,
coconut, sandalwood, yarrow

Leo

THE LION

July 23 – August 22

All About Leo

I f you want to get a sense of Leo's draw, imagine a magnet so strong that it not only pulls the nails out of your house but also every house in the neighborhood. The fifth sign of the zodiac is absolutely a star.

This tremendous magnetism has a tremendous ego to match. Justified or not, Leos think a lot of themselves. Not only do they love attention, they often demand it. Admiration, adoration, adulation—Leo feeds on it all. And when they don't get enough for whatever reason, they can suffer crushing waves of insecurity. Inside this mighty lion lives a tender soul.

Leo doesn't shy away from anything, least of all drama. In fact, this ambitious, boisterous sign might even court it. Exaggeration is good, but theatrics are better, goes the Leo line of reasoning. Frankly, though, what can you expect from a fire sign that's ruled by the sun? Being pulled into Leo's drama might be thrilling—just be careful about getting burned.

Things Leo Is Really Good At

When Leo talks, people listen. This sign is an entertaining performer and born leader. This same allure also helps Leo solve problems. Leos don't give up easily and ensure that no one else in their orbit does, either.

Ways Leos Can Stretch Themselves

As much as Leo craves approval, this sign has difficulty hearing—let alone heeding—the opinions of others. Having and expressing their own strong opinions should be balanced with listening to, and occasionally asking for, input.

Strengths and Weaknesses

STRENGTHS	WEAKNESSES
☐ Ambitious	☐ Egotistical
☐ Assured	☐ Fragile
☐ Fearless	☐ Insecure
☐ Generous	☐ Melodramatic
☐ High-spirited	☐ Overbearing
☐ Magnetic	☐ Unwilling to
☐ Optimistic	admit mistakes
	☐ Vain

ELEMENT

Fire

RULED BY

The Sun

COLORS

Burnt orange, copper, gold

GEMS AND MINERALS

Jacinth, peridot, pyrite

ANIMALS AND INSECTS

Cat, ladybug,
lion, peacock

PLANTS AND FLOWERS

Bromeliad, marigold,
sunflower

FAMOUS LEOS

Neil Armstrong, Kylie Jenner,
Daniel Dae Kim, Daniel Levy,
Jennifer Lopez, Madonna,
Meghan Markle, Andy Warhol

Friendship and Family

While everybody secretly imagines they're the star of their own movie, Leos genuinely believe they're the stars of everyone else's, too. The assumption that everyone is always watching makes them compassionate, patient, and warmhearted, with an attentive, generous manner. Being a good friend enhances their self-image.

Exhilarating to be around, Leo is typically the last person to leave the party. They radiate energy and exuberance, and have no problem beaming their delightful rays on family and friends. It's hard to be sad around them.

Leos tend to forgive easily, preferring to put their attention somewhere else (often themselves). Fiercely protective of their friends and family—their pride—Leos will grumble or growl at anyone who seems threatening.

But "pride" means more than their group of close friends; it also means their feelings. Leos bristle if anyone steals their spotlight. Allowing loved ones the chance to sparkle and dazzle once in a while can help strengthen and equalize relationships.

How to Get Along with Leo

- ☐ Agree (try not to argue!)
- ☐ Be über-generous with the compliments
- ☐ Stand back and let Leo bask in the spotlight

Signs Leo Gets Along With

Aries
Gemini
Libra
Sagittarius

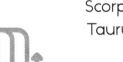

Signs Who Don't Always Get Leo

Aquarius
Scorpio
Taurus

Out and About

Leo loves a good outing. Leos thrive in the summer and are all about picnics, parties, concerts, and BBQs. Even in the winter, though, this social sign gets energized from the company of others, and they almost never lack for things to do. Practically a human sparkler, Leo brings the fun, whenever and wherever.

Reveling in their catlike nature, Leos won't turn down an opportunity to lie around relaxing (and looking pretty). But dangle the possibility of adventure in front of them, or hint at a surprise tailored just for them, and they'll be up and out the door . . . eventually.

The fact is that Leo won't leave the house without being 100 percent put together, even if it's just a trip to the gym or grocery store. Consider that when making plans with Leo and build some extra time into the invite.

Lucky Day	Lucky Number
Sunday	1

Activities Leo Enjoys

- ☐ Dancing
- ☐ Dressy occasions
- ☐ Hosting parties
- ☐ Makeup
- ☐ Performing
- ☐ Socializing
- ☐ Team sports

Things That Challenge Leo

- ☐ Anything mundane
- ☐ Being overshadowed or overlooked
- ☐ Dreariness
- ☐ Lacking an entourage
- ☐ Not being invited

Home and Away

As the self-proclaimed kings and queens of the zodiac, Leos long for a castle that befits their noble nature. Until they can re-create Versailles, though, they'll settle for doing whatever they can to make their home as opulent as possible. Everything looks pricey, even if it really isn't.

Leos happily welcome guests into their space, since doing so lets them present themselves and their lives in the most excellent light possible—quite literally. Plenty of mirrors reflect sunlight and show Leo off from every angle. But since Leos generally have better things to do than neaten up, be careful about peeking into their closets or under their beds.

On the road, Leo demonstrates the same intrepid spirit as at home. This sign prefers spontaneity and exploration over predictability and monotony. The best trip for Leo offers endless possibilities for action and excitement—and maybe, just maybe, Leo's travels will inspire a little envy in anyone left back home.

Where Is Leo Most at Home?

Leo is the happiest being at the center of the action, as in capital cities, or in exhilarating locales with nonstop spectacles. This sign likes places with exciting festivals, colorful scenery, and unmistakable, extraordinary dynamism.

Ways to Design Your Space to Align with Leo

☐ Go as opulent and lavish as you can afford
☐ Hang mirrors instead of art
☐ Design a gallery wall of favorite photos of you and your friends
☐ Accessorize with yellows, reds, and oranges to evoke warmth

Places Leo Definitely Needs to Travel To

☐ Accra, Ghana
☐ Bangkok, Thailand
☐ Barcelona, Spain
☐ Hollywood, California, United States
☐ Miami, Florida, United States
☐ New Orleans, Louisiana, United States
☐ Serengeti National Park, Tanzania

Health and Wellness

With so much pride and confidence, Leo tends to be image conscious. Their body is their temple, after all, so they put in the effort to exercise and eat right. Core exercises and cardio are particularly good for Leo, as this sign is prone to heart ailments and back injuries. Most of the time, however, Leo is powerful in body and in mind.

Leos want the glow they project from the inside to be matched by an equally radiant outside, so taking care of their skin and mane is often a top priority. Leo may be a sun sign, but that doesn't mean Leos should neglect sun safety. In addition to sunscreen, they should consider tucking that gorgeous hair under a hat.

Workouts that feel like capital-*E* events combat dullness and boredom, two things Leo hates. At the gym, as well as outside of it, Leo likes moving to music, particularly in the company of others.

Things That Nourish Leo

No sound makes Leos happier than applause; no words fill their hearts more than "you're amazing." Leo loves the expensive things in life, as befits someone so stately, such as fine clothes, sparkly jewels, or fancy chocolates.

Favorite Ways to Be Active

Barre workouts, horseback riding, spin classes, salsa dancing, soccer, Zumba

Ailments and Injuries to Watch Out For

Anger issues, back pain, high blood pressure, irregular heartbeat, narcissism, sciatica

Scents and Essential Oils

Cinnamon, ginger, juniper, lime, nutmeg, sweet orange

Virgo

THE MAIDEN

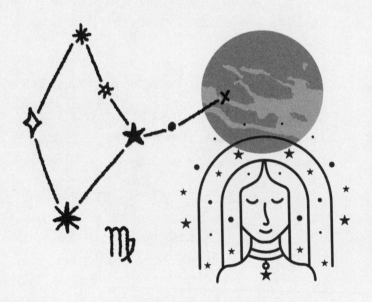

August 23 – September 22

All About Virgo

On the one hand, Virgo notices every flaw, every imperfection, every mistake. There's no hiding your coffee stain or mispronounced word from this sign. Observant, detail-oriented Virgo can be critical, no doubt. On the other hand, Virgos long to serve and to help others. When it comes to Virgo, making the world a better place isn't a marketing slogan but a life goal.

Luckily, Virgo has the chops to truly make a difference. This smart sign has a big intellect, desire for order, and willingness to work hard to effect real change. They are coolly logical and amazingly analytical. Sometimes this ability to leave emotion out of the equation is useful, as when thinking through a complex problem; sometimes it comes across as cold.

But the Virgo spirit is anything but chilly. Virgos give back out of the goodness of their heart. They aren't looking for adulation or adoration, although they appreciate a sincere thank-you, much like anyone else. Instead, this sign operates from a place of purehearted optimism. Virgo holds the world—and themselves—to certain standards. They are high standards, to be sure, yet Virgo believes that everyone has the power to meet them.

Things Virgo Is Really Good At

Virgo is associated with the harvest. This sign does an excellent job of sifting what's usable from what's not in many contexts, from managing information to analyzing data to finding workable solutions.

Ways Virgos Can Stretch Themselves

Conscientious Virgo can tip over into an obsession with details and flawlessness. The perfect is the enemy of the good. There comes a time when you have to hit "send," stop fiddling, put the red pen down, and move on.

Strengths and Weaknesses

STRENGTHS	WEAKNESSES
☐ Analytical	☐ Difficult
☐ Dedicated	☐ Fussy
☐ Diligent	☐ Haughty
☐ Intelligent	☐ Nervous
☐ Levelheaded	☐ Nitpicky
☐ Productive	☐ Self-effacing
☐ Thorough	☐ Uptight

ELEMENT

Earth

RULED BY

Mercury

COLORS

Light brown, mauve,
navy blue

GEMS AND MINERALS

Jade, sapphire, white topaz

ANIMALS AND INSECTS

Bee, chimpanzee, fox, raven

PLANTS AND FLOWERS

Aster, rubber plant,
sweet marjoram

FAMOUS VIRGOS

Kobe Bryant, Tim Burton,
Idris Elba, Salma Hayek,
Stephen King, Padma Lakshmi,
Keanu Reeves, Zendaya

Friendship and Family

Virgo might pass on an invite to your party but will almost certainly say yes when you ask for a ride to the airport or help finishing a project. Some people find Virgo aloof or snobbish, and there are definitely more outgoing members of the zodiac. The truth, though, is that this sign makes close friends easily, with a wonderful wit and refreshing unpretentiousness.

Once you have a Virgo friend, you have a friend for life. Virgos cultivate their friendships and care deeply about everyone in their surprisingly wide social circle.

Same goes for family, with Virgo often playing the role of caregiver. It's Virgo who checks that everyone has eaten, is wearing clean clothes, gets eight-plus hours of sleep per night, has finished their chores, etc. This practical sign deals in details and minutiae in a way that more larger-than-life signs might neglect. Depend on Virgo to pack the snacks, tissues, and hand sanitizer—and to anguish over whether you might run out.

How to Get Along with Virgo

- ☐ Be cool and calm
- ☐ Offer to join Virgo in helping out
- ☐ Say thank you
- ☐ Stay organized (don't be sloppy!)

Signs Virgo Gets Along With

Cancer
Capricorn
Scorpio
Taurus

Signs Who Don't Always Get Virgo

Gemini
Pisces
Sagittarius

Out and About

Virgos begin any day by looking at their carefully organized planner. This sign favors order, routine, and clear procedures. Don't make fun—Virgo gets stuff done, and staying organized helps.

Productivity is the key theme of the Virgo day (and life). This sign lives to work hard and accomplish goals. As such, the choice of every activity is carefully considered based on how useful it will be: doing a crossword helps grow their brain, for example, and going to see the hot movie everyone's talking about means they'll be able to chat about it the next day with their friends. Zoning out on video games, in contrast, isn't high on the Virgo to-do lists. (Yes, they have more than one to-do list.)

But Virgo is fairly OK when plans go off the rails. They are dependable, but they generally get that not everybody else is.

Lucky Day	Lucky Number
Wednesday	6

Activities Virgo Enjoys

- ☐ Chess
- ☐ Backpacking
- ☐ Board games
- ☐ Decluttering
- ☐ Gardening
- ☐ Photography
- ☐ Volunteering

Things That Challenge Virgo

- ☐ Being overly emotional
- ☐ Chaos
- ☐ Feeling useless
- ☐ Forgetfulness
- ☐ Loud noises
- ☐ Sloppiness
- ☐ Taking it easy

Home and Away

Wear nice socks when you head over to Virgo's place, since chances are good that it will be a "no shoe" house and you'll be asked to leave your kicks by the door. Virgo values cleanliness and neatness. *A lot.* Minor disorder will cause some concern; a big mess will cause a full-scale freak-out.

This meticulousness means that even the junk drawer will be organized into separate areas for loose rubber bands, stamps, and scissors. In the unlikely event that Virgo loses a phone charger, they'll be able to put their hands on a backup in no time.

Travel helps Virgo avoid the day-in, day-out doldrums. That said, Virgo is reluctant to go anywhere without a plan, and will research any trip until they're more or less an expert on the destination. A volunteering vacation with the potential for a positive impact, or a goal-oriented wellness trip, suits Virgo better than lounging around on a beach with an umbrella drink.

Where Is Virgo Most at Home?

As an earth sign, Virgo feels intimately connected to the natural world. Big landscapes can remind this sign to pull back and ease up on everyone, including themselves, once in a while.

Ways to Design Your Space to Align with Virgo

- ☐ Aim for functionality and practicality over fanciness
- ☐ Color-code your storage system
- ☐ Declutter daily (keep things neat!)
- ☐ Arrange vases of fresh flowers

Places Virgo Definitely Needs to Travel To

- ☐ The Himalayas, Asia
- ☐ Lapland, Finland
- ☐ Patagonia, Argentina and Chile
- ☐ Singapore
- ☐ Volcanoes National Park, Rwanda
- ☐ Zion National Park, Utah, United States

Health and Wellness

Virgos apply the same discrimination to their bodies as to the rest of their lives. This sign is careful about what they eat, careful to work out the right amount, and careful not to go to any extreme.

Yet Virgos can be nervous about their own health and seek medical advice on a fairly regular basis. Organized Virgo never misses a checkup, but could perhaps limit the in-between visits or follow-up messages unless absolutely necessary.

This same fastidiousness applies to their workouts. They are diligent and committed exercisers. However, Virgo perfectionism can cause them to be hard on themselves when they don't achieve a goal or get a new move down right away.

Industrious Virgo dislikes unproductive downtime, which often translates to neglecting to rest. But taking time to decompress—even if it needs to be scheduled weeks ahead of time—does wonders for Virgo.

Things That Nourish Virgo

Brainy Virgos like to learn new things because it enables them to be more useful to others. Completing a project that will benefit someone or something, be it a friend, a boss, or the planet, brings Virgo profound satisfaction.

Favorite Ways to Be Active

Bicycling, cross-country skiing, long-distance running and marathons, tai chi, TRX workouts

Ailments and Injuries to Watch Out For

Colitis, germaphobia, hypochondria, indigestion, irritable bowel syndrome, neurosis

Scents and Essential Oils

Eucalyptus, fennel, grapefruit, lemon, lily of the valley, sage

Libra

THE SCALES

September 23 – October 22

All About Libra

Some astrologers say the first six signs of the zodiac represent youth, adolescence, and young adulthood, while the second six represent middle age and beyond (see page 18 for the complete zodiac wheel). Libra, with its sense of refinement, willingness to compromise, and desire for harmony, can be seen as the first really grown-up sign.

Illustrated by the scales, Libra loves balance. But the two sides of the scales also hint at sometimes-competing personality traits. Libra is social and fun but dreadfully insecure, clever and capable but occasionally lazy. As laid-back as Libras are, they will fight (hard) for fairness. And while Libras like getting advice and soliciting opinions from others, they have trouble making decisions. When it comes to this sign, it's a little from column A, a little from column B.

Libras almost always look good. They love nice clothes, nice things, nice meals. Blessed with natural grace and plenty of allure, they make being attractive look enviably easy. With this talent, however, comes a dose of superficiality. There's no doubt that Libras are secretly judging us all.

Things Libra Is Really Good At

Obsessed with fairness, Libra follows the rules and doesn't hesitate to play referee, on the field or at work. This sign is passionate about equality, and Libras use their powers of persuasion to explain why everyone else should be as well.

Ways Libras Can Stretch Themselves

Thoughtful Libra wants to know everything before making a decision. Yet all too often, this quest leads to an almost paralyzing indecisiveness. While some decisions require careful thought, being impulsive and going with your first instinct can be incredibly freeing.

Strengths and Weaknesses

STRENGTHS	WEAKNESSES
☐ Accommodating	☐ Combative
☐ Approachable	☐ Dependent
☐ Diplomatic	☐ Fickle
☐ Fair	☐ Judgmental
☐ Rational	☐ Self-indulgent
☐ Refined	☐ Shallow

ELEMENT

Air

RULED BY

Venus

COLORS

Light blue, royal blue, white

GEMS AND MINERALS

Labradorite, opal,
pink tourmaline

ANIMALS AND INSECTS

Cicada, flamingo, lizard, swan

PLANTS AND FLOWERS

Hydrangea, monstera,
peace lily

FAMOUS LIBRAS

Donald Glover, Halsey, Isis King,
Bruno Mars, Alexandria Ocasio-Cortez,
Naomi Osaka, Gwyneth Paltrow,
Serena Williams

Friendship and Family

Libra's the sign of balance, and nothing balances an individual better than a partner. As such, Libra invests a lot in friendship. They ask their friends for advice, though they often wind up not taking it—not because they don't value the guidance but because they have trouble knowing when to stop getting input and start making a decision. Libra waffles.

Making decisions is one thing—making judgments, however, is no problem for Libra. A lover of beauty with excellent taste, this critical sign absolutely judges books by their covers. Others sometimes see Libra as superficial and stuck-up.

In the family, Libra usually plays peacemaker. Here's a sign who'll make sure everyone gets exactly the same amount of cake or an equal chance to pick which movie to watch next. Libra values harmony and civility, both of which foster a willingness to compromise.

How to Get Along with Libra

- ☐ Be patient during Libra's decision-making deliberations
- ☐ Give presents for no reason
- ☐ Have inside jokes
- ☐ Look good

Signs Libra Gets Along With

Aquarius
Gemini
Leo
Sagittarius

Signs Who Don't Always Get Libra

Aries
Cancer
Capricorn

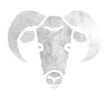

Out and About

Unsurprisingly, Libras work hard and play hard. The best days offer an equal mix of both, and often end with an evening out with friends.

How quickly Libra gets going in the morning depends on how late they were up the night before. But a late night out often gets offset by a cozy night in when Libra decides to curl up on the couch and read up on one of their many interests.

Libras take their indecisiveness wherever they go, including shopping. Rather than buy one sweater, they'll buy one in every color. They can be self-indulgent, especially when it comes to appearance. Post-shopping, Libra will want to eat at any restaurant known for beautiful food. The best meals for this image-conscious sign not only taste delicious but look amazing.

Lucky Day	Lucky Number
Friday	4

Activities Libra Enjoys

☐ Doing crossword puzzles
☐ Going to art museums
☐ Listening to music
☐ Rearranging and redecorating
☐ Skateboarding
☐ Spending money

Things That Challenge Libra

☐ Anarchy
☐ Discord
☐ Going solo
☐ Independence
☐ One-sidedness
☐ Shabbiness
☐ Ugliness

Home and Away

Libra likes a house that's both sophisticated and relaxing. It should be welcoming to guests and a place for Libra to recharge. The Libra home base provides an antidote to evenings out cavorting with friends. For Libras, balance is best.

Libras have no problem spending money on ideal items for their space. Like Taurus, Libra is ruled by Venus, goddess of beauty. Of all the signs, though, Libra knows best just how much people evaluate others based on what they're wearing, where they're living, or how they've decorated. Libras practice what they preach, and they make sure their own décor will stand up to anyone else's judgmental gaze.

Social Libra likes going to new places, especially big cities, with boundless culture and lots of options for entertainment. But Libra also feels pulled toward wide, open spaces, thanks to the air element of their nature. At heart, they're curious creatures and see the world as their oyster.

Where Is Libra Most at Home?

Cities offer the nonstop entertainment Libra loves, as well as the opportunity to banter with others wherever they go, whatever time of day. If the city is known for its gorgeous architecture or surrounded by a beautiful landscape, so much the better.

Ways to Design Your Space to Align with Libra

☐ Go for elegant furniture with clean lines
☐ Pick muted colors or neutrals, in keeping with Libra's sense of refinement
☐ Have at least one piece of statement art per room

☐ Aim for balance from room to room and within each room

Places Libra Definitely Needs to Travel To

☐ Cairo, Egypt
☐ Charleston, South Carolina, United States
☐ Dubrovnik, Croatia
☐ Jodhpur, India
☐ Lisbon, Portugal
☐ Mexico City, Mexico
☐ Montreal, Canada

Health and Wellness

This sign rules the skin, so Libras should be especially diligent about sunscreen and skin care. Seeing a dermatologist regularly can help with the sensitivity, dryness, and breakouts to which Libras are prone. So can drinking a lot of water, which has the additional benefit of flushing the kidneys, another body part ruled by Libra. Cranberry juice is good, too.

It probably goes without saying that Libras take time and care with their appearance, but they can fall prey to a tiny voice whispering that they might not be as wonderful as they think. Silencing this inner self-judgment takes practice. Libras can benefit from exercise that takes them out into nature and helps them get out of their own heads.

Because they feed off of positive reinforcement, such as friends telling them how great they are, people born under this sign don't enjoy being alone. More time with people amounts to more time to be admired. But Libra would do well to go beyond surfaces and try to find the beauty within.

Things That Nourish Libra

Spending time with friends in an elegant setting, perhaps over a cup of tea, makes the Libra soul sing. It's even better if the discussion dissects Libra's latest dilemma and gives everyone the chance to offer their take.

Favorite Ways to Be Active

Balance exercises, figure skating, gymnastics, partner yoga, surfing, working out with a personal trainer

Ailments and Injuries to Watch Out For

Acne and breakouts, appendicitis, crippling indecision, fear of being alone, obsessiveness, vindictiveness

Scents and Essential Oils

Almond, cyclamen, daffodil, freesia, geranium, pink pepper

Scorpio

THE SCORPION

October 23 – November 21

All About Scorpio

Scorpios enjoy extremes and love intensity. People born under this sign simply don't believe in doing anything halfway. Instead, they'd rather give their all—to games, to friends, to finding purpose and meaning—or nothing at all. They are resolute, emotional, and extreme. With an enthusiasm for sampling everything life has to offer, good and bad, Scorpios revel in being alive.

Among the symbols of Scorpio is the phoenix, the mythical bird that rises from the ashes. This is one powerful sign, super-mysterious and capable of transformation. They can be as enthralling as they are intimidating.

Few signs display such a high degree of introspection and intuition. Simply put, Scorpios understand themselves. They listen to their inner monologue and have a strong sense of their motivations, even if they don't often communicate those findings to others. This impressive self-awareness sometimes makes their behavior all the more puzzling. If they know they're capable of stinging so fiercely, why do they insist on doing it?

Things Scorpio Is Really Good At

Scorpios make excellent researchers and detectives, with extensive powers of perception and zero tolerance for nonsense. They're also quite funny, with wicked senses of humor.

Ways Scorpios Can Stretch Themselves

For a sign with such deep insights into themselves and others, Scorpios fear opening up. They prefer to keep most people at a cool remove. Sharing real feelings takes confidence as well as practice, but can ultimately make bonds stronger.

Strengths and Weaknesses

STRENGTHS	WEAKNESSES
☐ Devoted	☐ Easily angered
☐ Disciplined	☐ Hurtful
☐ Individualistic	☐ Jealous
☐ Insightful	☐ Melancholy
☐ Resilient	☐ Relentless
☐ Self-aware	☐ Secretive
☐ Witty	☐ Suspicious

ELEMENT

Water

RULED BY

Mars and Pluto

COLORS

Black, burgundy

GEMS AND MINERALS

Imperial topaz,
obsidian, smoky quartz

ANIMALS AND INSECTS

Eagle, scorpion,
snake, wolf

PLANTS AND FLOWERS

Cactus, dracaena, peony

FAMOUS SCORPIOS

Hillary Rodham Clinton,
Leonardo DiCaprio, Drake, Bill Gates,
Winona Ryder, Martin Scorsese,
Amandla Stenberg, SZA

Friendship and Family

When a Scorpio likes you, you've got a ride-or-die friend for life. This loyal sign loves as fervently, and with the same concentrated commitment, as it does pretty much everything else.

Because Scorpios don't reveal themselves easily, they expect a lot from anyone they've chosen to show their true selves to. This attitude can translate into possessiveness and jealousy if Scorpio starts to feel slighted in some way.

And beware the slighted Scorpio. It doesn't take much for this sign to lash out at even those they love most, including their family. They weaponize their sarcasm, they cut with criticism, and they attack with anger. When wounded or miserable, they want everyone else to feel equally wounded or miserable.

Most of the time, though, the potential benefits outweigh the sting. Scorpios drop everything to help a friend in need, and will listen, patiently and thoughtfully, to problems. They don't usually keep it light, and they don't expect their friends to, either—unless they're flashing their signature sarcastic wit. If that's the case, laugh away. Scorpio will.

How to Get Along with Scorpio

- ☐ Avoid prying into the Scorpio soul
- ☐ Be genuine
- ☐ Elevate sarcasm to an art form
- ☐ Give Scorpio your full attention (put your phone away!)

Signs Scorpio Gets Along With

Cancer
Capricorn
Pisces
Virgo

Signs Who Don't Always Get Scorpio

Aquarius
Leo
Taurus

Out and About

Setting an intention for the day helps Scorpio—even if said intention is as broad as planning to enjoy whatever comes their way. They need to feel as if they're actively living their lives, not passing the time. Plus, even the most outgoing Scorpio craves solitude and space before setting forth into the world, stinger locked and loaded.

Intuitive and individualistic, Scorpios seek a range of experiences in keeping with their emotional nature. One day, this could mean free-soloing or white-water rafting; another day, it could mean settling into a hammock and contemplating the meaning of life. Scorpio goes deep, even when relaxing.

Feeling alive means being in touch with every sense and every emotion. And, for Scorpio, feeling most alive often equals feeling totally exhilarated. You'll frequently find this sign capping the day off by watching the scariest of scary movies.

Lucky Day	Lucky Number
Tuesday	7

Activities Scorpio Enjoys

- ☐ Astrology
- ☐ Being introspective
- ☐ Exploring and traveling
- ☐ Keeping secrets
- ☐ Solving mysteries
- ☐ Watching movies
- ☐ Yoga

Things That Challenge Scorpio

- ☐ Being stuck in a rut
- ☐ Betrayal
- ☐ Conformity
- ☐ Cowardice
- ☐ Powerlessness
- ☐ Small talk
- ☐ Superficiality

Home and Away

Scorpios thrive in an environment that stimulates every sense. They need good smells, colorful art, killer music, silky fabrics, and a snack plate full of spicy treats. They hunger, thirst, want, and yearn. So they feel most at home in a place that satisfies their various appetites.

Regardless of their living situation, Scorpios need a zone that's truly theirs. It could be a bedroom or an office, a nook or an alcove, but it needs to belong to them fully and utterly. Think of it as the physical manifestation of their secretive, private side. No peeking, no sharing.

Scorpios adore traveling. Visiting new places lets them tap into both their thinking and feeling sides. Generally, though, Scorpios prefer spending time in one spot, or at least traveling slowly. They're not wild about the quick trip and would rather nestle in, allowing a place's nuances to gradually be revealed.

Where Is Scorpio Most at Home?

Like their sign siblings, Cancer and Pisces, Scorpios love the water. They particularly like transition zones, such as estuaries and swamps, which are filled with life and speak to the transformative nature of Scorpio.

Ways to Design Your Space to Align with Scorpio

- ☐ Make it unique—a Scorpio space should feel like the individual who lives there
- ☐ Search flea markets for one-of-a-kind vintage finds
- ☐ Pick darker colors or wallpaper for an accent wall
- ☐ Hang blackout curtains to create a private retreat

Places Scorpio Definitely Needs to Travel To

- ☐ Alaska, United States
- ☐ Hạ Long Bay, Vietnam
- ☐ Iguazú Falls, Argentina and Brazil
- ☐ Lake Natron, Tanzania
- ☐ Shanghai, China
- ☐ Transylvania, Romania

Health and Wellness

Scorpio uses vigorous physical activity to process powerful feelings. A competitive side drives them to the front row of every exercise class—and keeps them practicing until they could probably sub for the teacher.

Given their all-in tendencies, Scorpios sometimes fall into unhealthy habits or behaviors. They may exercise or work to the point of exhaustion, for example. When it comes to health, Scorpios need to guard against excesses. Same goes for risks and dares. Go ahead and experience whatever life has to offer, Scorpio, but remember to do so safely.

The famed Scorpio intuition applies to the Scorpio mind and body. This sign knows what it needs to function best. Scorpios do not wait to deal with problems or flip-flop once they've settled on a solution. They demonstrate remarkable inner strength and resilience.

Things That Nourish Scorpio

This intense sign feeds on intensity. Scorpios like bold flavors and edgy experiences, pushing boundaries and feeling all the feelings. If it seems a bit scary to another sign, it's probably super-fun for Scorpio.

Favorite Ways to Be Active

Archery, elliptical training, hatchet throwing, kickboxing, Krav Maga, Muay Thai, trapeze

Ailments and Injuries to Watch Out For

Avoidance anxiety, constipation, extreme secrecy, fatigue, jealousy, lying

Scents and Essential Oils

Anise, cedarwood, gardenia, hyacinth, jasmine, rose, wisteria

Sagittarius

THE ARCHER

November 22 – December 21

All About Sagittarius

Sagittarius is the *zzziiiipppp* of a suitcase being closed, the *whoosh* of an airplane taking off, the *thunk* of a passport being stamped. People born under this sign were born to roam. Watch them go.

Wild Sagittarius doesn't want to be tamed and can't stand being hemmed in. In love with the open road and infatuated with freedom, Sagittariuses dislike commitment and confinement, preferring to keep options open for as long as possible. They get fidgety.

Yet Sagittarius has another side, seeking out spiritual knowledge with diligence and concentration. Smart Sagittarius searches for deeper meaning through travels, education, and conversation. They make patient teachers, not to mention talented storytellers. Thanks to their travels, most Sagittariuses have a stockpile of jokes and wacky anecdotes.

Even though they're friendly, entertaining, and personable, Sagittariuses still bump up against saying "the right thing." They prefer radical honesty. Sagittariuses simply cannot keep their comments to themselves—not that they try very hard. Instead, they pretty much always feel compelled to speak with candor, even when kindness or silence might be more appropriate.

Things Sagittarius Is Really Good At

Ever the optimist, Sagittarius lives with an infectious idealism. This sign inspires others—in every possible way—whether they are helping friends broaden their horizons, commit to a plan, explore an exotic destination, or break free of blind obedience.

Ways Sagittariuses Can Stretch Themselves

Sagittarius has a childlike innocence when it comes to revealing the truth about people or situations. This sign operates from a place of honesty, never mean-spiritedness. However, a little tact could prevent Sagittarius from unintentionally wounding others.

Strengths and Weaknesses

STRENGTHS	WEAKNESSES
☐ Broad-minded	☐ Careless
☐ Cheerful	☐ Disorganized
☐ Good-humored	☐ Distractable
☐ Honest	☐ Imprecise
☐ Inquisitive	☐ Naïve
☐ Positive	☐ Rude
☐ Unpretentious	☐ Wishy-washy

ELEMENT
Fire

RULED BY
Jupiter

COLORS
Orange, purple

GEMS AND MINERALS
Lepidolite, sugilite, turquoise

ANIMALS AND INSECTS
Firefly, horse,
owl, zebra

PLANTS AND FLOWERS
Carnation, coleus,
dandelion

FAMOUS SAGITTARIUSES
Jane Austen, Walt Disney,
Jimi Hendrix, Nicholas Hoult,
Scarlett Johansson, Nicki Minaj,
Janelle Monáe, Taylor Swift

Friendship and Family

Popular Sagittarius brings an open mind and free spirit to friendship. As a result, Sagittariuses have wide circles of friends and acquaintances. This sign makes connections easily, welcoming one and all to come hang out or join them on their next escapade.

In conversation, Sagittariuses like to ramble widely and freely, just like in their travels. They have an excellent, almost zany sense of humor and enjoy practical jokes. All their travels give them plenty of good stories. Still, this sign doesn't shy away from discussing heavier topics, in line with their love of spirituality, wisdom, and philosophy.

A desire to be perceived as cool coupled with a total lack of a filter means sometimes Sagittarius says the wrong thing. At best, they could work on developing some tact, or teaching themselves to think before they blurt. At worst, they can be downright rude, even cutting. Honesty is not always the best policy.

How to Get Along with Sagittarius

- ☐ Be a free spirit
- ☐ Enjoy being outdoors
- ☐ Laugh a lot
- ☐ Like sports
- ☐ Tell great jokes

Signs Sagittarius Gets Along With

Aquarius
Aries
Leo
Libra

Signs Who Don't Always Get Sagittarius

Gemini
Pisces
Virgo

Out and About

With their trademark enthusiasm, Sagittariuses turn the most ordinary of walks into an opportunity for noticing and discovering. As such, life with Sagittarius is rarely boring. Trust Sagittarius to find a lovely pocket park or excellent café in a neighborhood you've been to a thousand times. Sagittarius can always teach you something new about a place you think you know.

Sagittariuses love planning, since that's when the possibilities seem most boundless. Everything and anything is imaginable at the start. Follow-through, however, can be trickier, since that's when one starts to bump against rules and limits, two things that damper the Sagittarius spirit. Their enthusiasm flags.

An ideal Sagittarius day includes time spent outdoors and time spent stretching their brain, preferably with a friend they can talk to and compare insights with. The day, or night, should also include at least one experience that expands the mind of these wisdom seekers in a meaningful way.

Lucky Day	Lucky Number
Thursday	3

Activities Sagittarius Enjoys

- ☐ Camping
- ☐ Horseback riding
- ☐ Playing and watching sports
- ☐ Speaking freely
- ☐ Traveling
- ☐ Watching documentaries and travel shows

Things That Challenge Sagittarius

- ☐ Confinement
- ☐ Dependence
- ☐ Excessive rules
- ☐ Ignorance
- ☐ Illness
- ☐ Lies
- ☐ Running out of places to go

Home and Away

If ever a sign were meant to travel, it's Sagittarius. Symbolized by an archer, Sagittariuses like to fly, roam, wander, and explore. No destination in mind? No problem. No place to stay when you get there? No worries. Sagittariuses love all trips, big or small, and don't sweat the details.

Unfortunately, though, details need to be sweated, tickets purchased, accommodations selected, and so on. Restless Sagittariuses would do well to stop and concentrate on the small things, rather than leaving that work for others.

At home, Sagittarius demands space and freedom. Even when forced indoors, Sagittariuses will be at the window, admiring their beloved natural world and fantasizing about their next big trip.

Where Is Sagittarius Most at Home?

This sign loves being outside, especially under a big sky or looking at a limitless horizon. At the same time, though, Sagittariuses have a spiritual side that feels at home in sacred places.

Ways to Design Your Space to Align with Sagittarius

- ☐ Use wood and natural fabrics for a rustic atmosphere
- ☐ Display quirky souvenirs and mementos from past trips
- ☐ Avoid anything that looks matchy-matchy
- ☐ Grow a plant wall to help bring the outdoors in

Places Sagittarius Definitely Needs to Travel To

- ☐ Angkor Wat, Cambodia
- ☐ Budapest, Hungary
- ☐ Glacier National Park, Montana, United States
- ☐ Iceland
- ☐ Jerusalem, Israel
- ☐ Kruger National Park, South Africa
- ☐ Machu Picchu, Peru
- ☐ New Zealand

Health and Wellness

With an instinctive love of sports, Sagittariuses are often excellent athletes. And yet, this sign is particularly prone to clumsiness and accidents. Even as Sagittarius seeks adventure across the horizon, this sign would be wise to literally look before they leap.

In their never-ending pursuit of adventure, Sagittariuses don't always notice when they're starting to get run down. People born under this sign could do a better job of listening to their bodies. As they're planning their next epic journey, they should consider situations that might cause stress, strain, or pain and plan ahead.

This sign rules the hips and thighs, so those areas often get tight, especially after a day of nonstop wandering. In addition to regular stretching, laughter lifts the Sagittarius spirit, and they want those around them to laugh, too.

Things That Nourish Sagittarius

In keeping with their wanderlust, Sagittariuses love trying unfamiliar foods, exploring unfamiliar places, meeting people, and packing their brain full of ideas. It's knowledge they're after, and knowledge that sustains them.

Favorite Ways to Be Active

Belly dancing, CrossFit, fusion classes,
long-distance running, parkour,
rock climbing, roller-skating

Ailments and Injuries to Watch Out For

Agitation, claustrophobia, clumsiness,
hip pain, immaturity, procrastination

Scents and Essential Oils

Cardamom, iris, myrrh, peach,
saffron, tea tree, violet

Capricorn

THE GOAT

December 22–January 19

All About Capricorn

Capricorns are the masters of self-control. This trait helps them overcome any obstacle in pursuit of their goals. Like their zodiac animal, the goat, Capricorns doggedly climb and diligently scramble. They conquer, they achieve, they rise to the top.

Such self-control gives Capricorn sensibility and practicality. They are capable, enterprising, and meticulous. But it also gives them a stuffy, traditional side, one that submits to authority and worships convention. "That's not how it's done" might well be the Capricorn mantra.

Capricorn definitely has a parental vibe going. This is the calm, stable sign you want on hand during a crisis, or the sign you call when you need help with something dreary but necessary, like doing your taxes. "Parent mode" lets Capricorn cut through the nonsense and do what needs to be done. At the same time, Capricorns can be obsessed with rules and concerned with what the neighbors might think. A drop of dreaminess once in a while, or a dollop of spontaneity, would help Capricorn loosen up.

Things Capricorn Is Really Good At

Plenty of signs dream big, but steady, detail-oriented Capricorn has the follow-through to see their goals all the way to completion. This sign accepts responsibility and takes pride in maintaining traditions.

Ways Capricorns Can Stretch Themselves

Capricorns can be straightlaced and serious, prudent and perseverant. Coupled with hard work, these qualities get the job done. Nevertheless, this sign could stand to cut loose and have fun once in a while.

Strengths and Weaknesses

STRENGTHS	WEAKNESSES
☐ Careful	☐ Calculating
☐ Commonsensical	☐ Condescending
☐ Goal-oriented	☐ Conventional
☐ Hardworking	☐ Opportunistic
☐ Methodical	☐ Overbearing
☐ Perseverant	☐ Pessimistic
☐ Self-reliant	☐ Unyielding

ELEMENT
Earth

RULED BY
Saturn

COLORS
Dark brown, forest green

GEMS AND MINERALS
Amber, chrysoprase, howlite

ANIMALS AND INSECTS
Beaver, deer, goat, silkworm

PLANTS AND FLOWERS
Bonsai, pothos, shepherd's purse

FAMOUS CAPRICORNS
Timothée Chalamet, Martin Luther King Jr., LeBron James, Julia Louis-Dreyfus, Lin-Manuel Miranda, Dolly Parton, Elvis Presley, Greta Thunberg

Friendship and Family

Regardless of their actual age, most Capricorns seem to have bypassed youthful follies and landed squarely in adulthood. They make stable, mature, authentic friends, the kind of person you turn to in emergencies or when you most need to get something done.

When it comes to getting things done, Capricorns prefer to go it alone. But Capricorn still cherishes friends and family, even if this sign doesn't go in for the mushy stuff.

Capricorns can be rigid; they like rules. Before anyone criticizes or judges, they would do well to remember that we need rules—without them, we'd all be spinning around in utter chaos like toddlers at a candy buffet.

Standing and reputation matter to Capricorn. People born under this sign long to be admired, especially for their achievements and efforts. They want respect, but, with their diligence and productivity, they've usually earned it.

How to Get Along with Capricorn

- ☐ Applaud Capricorn's efforts and accomplishments
- ☐ Be successful in your own right
- ☐ Obey the rules
- ☐ Stay calm

Signs Capricorn Gets Along With

Pisces
Scorpio
Taurus
Virgo

Signs Who Don't Always Get Capricorn

Aries
Cancer
Libra

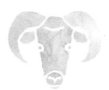

Out and About

ACapricorn day is an organized day, and likely similar to the day before (and the day to follow). Predictability makes this sign feel secure. Spontaneity makes this sign anxious.

That daily routine certainly includes work. Capricorns are the workhorses of the zodiac, the sign that puts the *i* in industry. Even weekends will likely include some toil or labor, whether that's around the house or out performing good deeds in the community. They give back, in part because they like the praise that comes with doing so.

Relaxing doesn't come easily to this sign. Capricorn hobbies, such as they are, need to have a tangible result—painting, playing music, baking, or DIY projects make good choices, if Capricorns can pull themselves away from the grind. It's a big "if."

Hard work coupled with ambition often leads to Capricorn career success. They earn, then stick that money in the bank. Frugal and farsighted, they tend to be excellent savers.

Lucky Day	Lucky Number
Saturday	5

Activities Capricorn Enjoys

- ☐ Card games
- ☐ Carpentry/DIY projects
- ☐ Day-trading
- ☐ Decorating for the holidays (upholding family traditions)
- ☐ Genealogy
- ☐ Playing an instrument

Things That Challenge Capricorn

- ☐ Breaking the rules
- ☐ Emoting
- ☐ Indulgence
- ☐ Losing control
- ☐ Pandemonium
- ☐ Spontaneity
- ☐ Unstructured time

Home and Away

Capricorns believe in quality over quantity, and they have a definite frugal streak. As a result, their homes feel classic and timeless, neat and organized. There's no chaos here, no flimsy bookcases or cobbled-together coffee tables. There are, however, numerous work spaces, with great task lighting and accessible docking stations.

This sign likes earthy colors, which offer a feeling of groundedness. The Capricorn home is a place of stability and security. Photos and awards show off Capricorn triumphs.

As mature, responsible types, Capricorns pack multiple maps and guidebooks whenever they travel. They not only print itineraries but enclose them in plastic sleeves so nothing gets damaged. You'll find this sign on the beaten path, asking the tour guide questions, then cross-checking answers against previously completed research.

Where Is Capricorn Most at Home?

As an earth sign, Capricorn does well in places that seem solid and unchanging, like mountains or historic sites. Capricorns also have a profound connection to trees and forests.

Ways to Design Your Space to Align with Capricorn

- ☐ Buy the nicest pieces you can afford
- ☐ Add some antiques or family heirlooms
- ☐ Layer on the earth tones, especially brown
- ☐ Hang up degrees or accolades
- ☐ Keep it classic

Places Capricorn Definitely Needs to Travel To

- ☐ Boston, Massachusetts, United States
- ☐ Cyprus
- ☐ Lalibela, Ethiopia
- ☐ Mount Everest, Nepal and Tibet
- ☐ Redwood National and State Parks, California, United States
- ☐ Stonehenge, United Kingdom
- ☐ Torres del Paine National Park, Chile
- ☐ Vatican City

Health and Wellness

Alongside Capricorn's legendary work ethic goes a legendary tolerance for stress. While a little stress can provide a sense of urgency and spur productivity, too much stress can lead to significant issues. For Capricorn, work is generally considered to be the solution to most problems. Capricorn needs to guard against an unhealthy amount of adrenaline and pressure.

Exercise helps, and Capricorns love structure and repetition. A favorite route or routine fills this sign with a sense of comfort and confidence, not boredom or monotony. Capricorns want to see results and benefits, so they often keep track of number of miles or reps to see what should be adjusted.

This practical approach extends to self-care. Capricorns prefer progress they can track. Otherwise, the self-care attempt will get shunted aside in favor of something else. Scents and essential oils can be a quick and efficient way to help this sign relax.

Things That Nourish Capricorn

Capricorns need to see results, even during downtime, so this sign enjoys activities with measurable accomplishments, such as hiking to the top of a mountain, weeding a garden, converting a garage into a home gym, or baking the world's best banana bread.

Favorite Ways to Be Active

Ballet, diving, hockey, jogging, kayaking,
mountaineering, power walking

Ailments and Injuries to Watch Out For

Anxiety, bone fractures, osteoporosis,
overwork, perfectionism, tooth decay

Scents and Essential Oils

Angelica, cumin, oakwood, pine,
sweetgrass, teakwood, thyme, tulip

Aquarius

THE WATER BEARER

January 20 – February 18

All About Aquarius

Count yourself lucky to have an Aquarius in your life. This sign is one of a kind, a true original, a creative inventor and innovative thinker. Indeed, Aquariuses are often considered to be the smartest members of the zodiac.

But the Aquarian big intellect doesn't leave much room for emotion. Aquariuses have little patience for feelings, whether their own or someone else's. At their most extreme, people born under this sign can act like extraterrestrials on a temporary earthly sojourn. They happily live in their heads or on their gadgets, with zero interest in conforming or being anyone other than their eccentric selves.

For a sign that can be independent to the point of rebelliousness, Aquariuses have an enormous humanitarian streak. They care about community. Big believers in tolerance and committed to social responsibility, they make dedicated advocates for diversity, equity, and inclusion.

Aquariuses tend to be cheery, in part because this positive energy helps others go along with their often unorthodox ideas. If anyone can come up with a solution to society's most pressing problems—and get everyone on the planet on board—it's Aquarius.

Things Aquarius Is Really Good At

Where most people see only problems, Aquariuses see possibilities. With a firm focus on the future, this sign loves to imagine, invent, experiment, innovate, create, and discover what comes next.

Ways Aquariuses Can Stretch Themselves

Community-minded Aquarius could do a better job one-on-one. This sign sometimes feels superior to others and doesn't hesitate to show it. Yet gaining consensus often starts with connecting on an individual level, and occasionally even compromising.

Strengths and Weaknesses

STRENGTHS	WEAKNESSES
☐ Articulate	☐ Aloof
☐ Future-oriented	☐ Childish
☐ Inventive	☐ Disconnected
☐ Logical	☐ High-strung
☐ Philanthropic	☐ Insensitive
☐ Progressive	☐ Rebellious
☐ Tolerant	☐ Thoughtless

ELEMENT

Air

RULED BY

Saturn and Uranus

COLORS

Electric blue, sky blue

GEMS AND MINERALS

Fluorite, lapis lazuli, sodalite

ANIMALS AND INSECTS

Axolotl, otter,
pangolin, water strider

PLANTS AND FLOWERS

Orchid, rex begonia,
string of pearls

FAMOUS AQUARIUSES

Elizabeth Banks, Henry Golding,
Tom Hiddleston, Alicia Keys,
Toni Morrison, Questlove,
Cristiano Ronaldo, Harry Styles

Friendship and Family

Given the name (Aquarius) and symbol (Water Bearer), it's easy to confuse an Aquarius for an emotional water sign. Easy, that is, until you meet one in person. The truth is that this air sign prefers thoughts over feelings, ideas over emotions, deeds over empathy. Other signs will give you hugs; Aquariuses will give you solutions.

Despite not wanting to deal with feelings, Aquariuses attract a big, diverse group of friends. Broad-minded and tolerant, they believe in celebrating everyone's uniqueness, much as they revel in their own. Conformists need not apply.

Anyone can bump against Aquarian stubbornness, but friends and family are especially familiar with this sign's obstinacy. Aquariuses simply won't budge when asked to compromise or make concessions about who they are or what they believe. Nonetheless, Aquariuses tend to be very cheerful and very kind—and perhaps this cheery kindness is the secret to this sign so often getting its way.

How to Get Along with Aquarius

- ☐ Care about social responsibility
- ☐ Display your eccentricities
- ☐ Live ethically
- ☐ Value what makes Aquarius unique

Signs Aquarius Gets Along With

Aries
Gemini
Libra
Sagittarius

Signs Who Don't Always Get Aquarius

Leo
Scorpio
Taurus

Out and About

In their head as they may be, Aquariuses nevertheless enjoy getting out and exploring. They want to see how issues are played out in the real world, adding to their mental database of what needs fixing. After all, they can't create, invent, or tweak something they don't understand.

Volunteering lets Aquarius give back in an effective, concrete way. Their humanitarianism spurs them to become involved with various charities or nonprofits, while their progressiveness and tolerance make them advocates for real change in their communities.

Rational, logical Aquariuses love to discuss. They rely on their characteristic friendliness to initiate conversation with just about anyone, but they have trouble dropping an argument once it's begun. Don't bother asking them to compromise, either.

Aquarius could not care less about accomplishments or status, with one exception: culture. This sign is in the front row of the avant-garde music festival, all in at any exhibition exploring science and technology, and first in line at the sci-fi film festival.

Lucky Day	Lucky Number
Wednesday	12

Activities Aquarius Enjoys

- ☐ Astronomy
- ☐ Coding
- ☐ Logic and puzzles
- ☐ Making digital art
- ☐ Playing video games
- ☐ Trying different life hacks

Things That Challenge Aquarius

- ☐ Compromise
- ☐ Convention
- ☐ Ennui
- ☐ Histrionics
- ☐ Intolerance
- ☐ Limitations
- ☐ Looking backward

Home and Away

At home, Aquariuses want to be connected and prepared for inspiration to strike at any time, so they keep their cherished devices near at hand, with chargers everywhere. Overall, their space exudes a clean, minimalist vibe. High-quality plastics, metals, and glass lend an ultramodern effect.

Don't be surprised if Aquarius renovates even a rented apartment—this sign needs a home to be as distinctive and singular as they are.

With a strong interest in the future, Aquariuses like technology and believe in its power to make our lives better. Their travel gear might look like it's out of a movie about high-tech spies, but it helps this sign avoid inconveniences, such as excessively chatty seatmates or spotty connectivity. Aquarius tends to be light-years ahead of the rest of us.

Where Is Aquarius Most at Home?

Until Aquarius can easily get to the moon, this sign will make do with experiencing otherworldly places on earth, particularly those with striking landscapes. Aquariuses also like futuristic, tech-focused cities.

Ways to Design Your Space to Align with Aquarius

- ☐ Opt for minimalism over maximalism
- ☐ Pick modular pieces in plastic, metal, or glass
- ☐ Incorporate the latest technology

Places Aquarius Definitely Needs to Travel To

- ☐ Abu Dhabi, United Arab Emirates
- ☐ Beijing, China
- ☐ Helsinki, Finland
- ☐ Nairobi, Kenya
- ☐ Richat Structure, Mauritania
- ☐ Seoul, South Korea
- ☐ Silicon Valley, California, United States
- ☐ Vermilion Cliffs National Monument, Arizona, United States

Health and Wellness

Some signs exercise because they love the way it makes their body feel; other signs exercise because they know—intellectually—that exercise brings about major benefits. Aquariuses tend to fall into the latter camp, recognizing that a healthy body helps the brain go.

Aquariuses seem as equally suited to solitary pursuits as to team sports. Alone, of course, they get to stay fully focused on whatever project or scheme is bubbling within them. Their constant internal calculations make them excellent strategists on the field, too, and their emotional detachment turns them into formidable opponents.

On the outside, Aquarius stays cool and collected. Inside, however, might be an entirely different situation. Aquariuses are reluctant to process, let alone reveal, their emotional side—but they do have one, of course. Finding productive ways to deal with feelings is a necessary challenge for this sign.

Things That Nourish Aquarius

People born under this sign have a huge array of interests and causes that gives their lives shape and purpose. So while the specifics might differ, Aquariuses share a love of philanthropy as well as a distinct individuality. They enjoy being themselves.

Favorite Ways to Be Active

Aerial yoga, badminton,
isometric exercise, stair-climbing,
trampoline, trapeze, windsurfing

Ailments and Injuries to Watch Out For

Anemia, difficulty with social interactions,
emotional detachment, shin splints,
sprained ankle, varicose veins

Scents and Essential Oils

Black pepper, chrysanthemum, hemp,
lemon verbena, licorice root, lotus

Pisces

TWO FISH

February 19 – March 20

All About Pisces

The zodiac begins with Aries, fiery and brave, and ends with Pisces, dreamy and imaginative. Pisces walk with their feet on the ground but their head in the clouds. They have a romantic, otherworldly air about them.

Few signs have such an artistic spirit. The act of creation helps bridge the two worlds in which Pisces seem to dwell. They paint, they draw, they write poems and songs. Just don't expect Pisces to take out the trash or be on time. They have other concerns.

Pisces feels—intensely, effusively, utterly. This sign absorbs energy and emotions from everything it sees, hears, talks to, touches, smells, and experiences. Such empathy makes Pisces a caring, devoted person, someone who is unfailingly kind and unstintingly compassionate.

But this spongelike sensitivity can take away from the Piscean sense of self. Pisces tends to absorb, rather than act. People born under this sign are often passive. If not careful, they can lose themselves to those with bolder, more assertive personalities.

Things Pisces Is Really Good At

A sign this in tune with dreams and vibes naturally inhabits a detailed fantasy world, and this translates into imaginative creations. Pisces are among astrology's most prolific poets, artists, filmmakers, musicians, and creators.

Ways Pisces Can Stretch Themselves

Putting up boundaries simply isn't the Piscean way. This sign takes in everybody's everything. But it's important to have at least some boundaries, as being so attuned to others can lead to Pisces being controlled by someone else's wishes or will.

Strengths and Weaknesses

STRENGTHS	WEAKNESSES
☐ Artistic	☐ Absentminded
☐ Compassionate	☐ Escapist
☐ Perceptive	☐ Gullible
☐ Romantic	☐ Impractical
☐ Supportive	☐ Indirect
☐ Sympathetic	☐ Passive
☐ Unselfish	☐ Self-negating

ELEMENT

Water

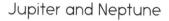

RULED BY

Jupiter and Neptune

COLORS

Aqua, sea green, turquoise

GEMS AND MINERALS

Aquamarine, clear quartz, pearl

ANIMALS AND INSECTS

Dolphin, elephant,
fish, moth

PLANTS AND FLOWERS

Spider plant, water lily, ZZ plant

FAMOUS PISCES

Ruth Bader Ginsburg,
Justin Bieber, Simone Biles,
Albert Einstein, Spike Lee,
Lupita Nyong'o, Elliot Page,
Elizabeth Taylor

Friendship and Family

People flock to Pisces, correctly sensing in this sign a willingness to sympathize. Pisces, in turn, offer their renowned kindness and compassion to one and all. But Pisces might not be as extroverted as they first appear. In fact, they tend to have a small circle of truly close friends, surrounded by ring after ring of casual acquaintances.

These close friends—some of which go back to childhood—often become members of the Piscean family. Faithful Pisces dote on their crew. They empathize with everyone but adore their besties and families.

Being friends with, or related to, a Pisces comes with a distinct responsibility. After all, these people see firsthand just how sensitive this sign can be. They've witnessed Pisces become overwhelmed with worry or crippled by the effort of dispensing such care and consideration to everyone. So they have to do what they can to not add to the Piscean burden or take advantage of the Piscean benevolence.

How to Get Along with Pisces

☐ Be practical and grounded
☐ Compliment Piscean creations
☐ Show your sentimental side
☐ Talk about your dreams

Signs Pisces Gets Along With

Cancer
Capricorn
Scorpio
Taurus

Signs Who Don't Always Get Pisces

Gemini
Sagittarius
Virgo

Out and About

Most of the time, affable Pisces thrives in the wide world. When others are happy, they're happy. They like concerts, social events, watching sports, or just hanging out. The perfect Piscean day involves spending time with joyful people.

By the same token, when others are unhappy, Pisces becomes unhappy. Ditto if someone gets annoyed, angry, embarrassed, anxious, afraid—the list goes on. This sign is preternaturally disposed to take on whatever feelings are floating around in its vicinity, much like a tablecloth stained by a spilled drink or a city cloaked in a fog. The negative emotion seeps in and transforms Pisces.

Eventually, this sign will need to escape. Sometimes Pisces simply escape into their mind, and use their imagination to rewrite the situation. And sometimes they need to literally escape and head home.

Lucky Day	Lucky Number
Friday	8

Activities Pisces Enjoys

- ☐ Daydreaming
- ☐ Magic
- ☐ Making art and music
- ☐ Role-playing games
- ☐ Sailing
- ☐ Swimming
- ☐ Tarot reading

Things That Challenge Pisces

- ☐ Apathy
- ☐ Being landlocked
- ☐ Hostility
- ☐ Lack of imagination
- ☐ Practicality
- ☐ Remoteness
- ☐ Teasing

Home and Away

When the world gets to be too much, Pisces needs a place to decompress. As such, the Piscean home tends to be comfortable, with lots of areas for lounging, inside and out. The squishier and softer, the better. Everything, from the lines of the furniture to the artwork, exudes a feeling of well-being and calm.

As you might expect from a water sign that's represented by fish, Pisces functions best when close to water. While views are delightful, Pisces will settle for aquariums, fountains, even photos of rivers and oceans. They might paint their walls with blocks or stripes of blue, or decorate with coral, sea glass, and wicker.

In keeping with the water theme, cruises make an ideal Piscean trip. Not only does a cruise let Pisces indulge its love of the sea, but it also lets this sign cede control of the planning and details. All Pisces needs to do is relax.

Where Is Pisces Most at Home?

A true water sign, Pisces loves to be near lakes, rivers, and especially oceans. The tide echoes their own journey back and forth from this world to another, from the tangible to the intangible, from everyone else to themselves.

Ways to Design Your Space to Align with Pisces

- ☐ Try an ombré wall treatment in shades of blue
- ☐ Designate a place for creating or daydreaming
- ☐ Arrange pillows and blankets for maximum lounging

Places Pisces Definitely Needs to Travel To

- ☐ Antarctica
- ☐ The Bahamas
- ☐ Cartagena, Colombia
- ☐ Casablanca, Morocco
- ☐ Fiji
- ☐ Salar de Uyuni, Bolivia
- ☐ Seattle, Washington, United States
- ☐ Wales, United Kingdom

Health and Wellness

Living such a rich fantasy life sometimes causes Pisces to forget about their actual life. Sometimes they need to be nudged or reminded to exercise, much like they need to be nudged or reminded to pay bills, put the gas cap back on, take their keys out of the door . . . Pisces can be absentminded and forgetful.

A common knock on Pisces is that this sign is lazy. Not so! The fact is that being as empathetic as Pisces can wear a person down. Soaking up the world's feelings takes effort and energy. Understandably, Pisces needs to recharge. In this case, chilling is a form of self-care, not a sign of laziness.

Speaking of reclining, Pisces rules the feet. So a pedicure, foot massage, or good old-fashioned soak with some Epsom salts might be a nice way to replenish a sagging soul or combat aching toes.

Things That Nourish Pisces

Pisces cherish their fantasies. Imagination is their default setting. They draw on this side of themselves to create and express their personality. In addition to artistic pursuits, Pisces often find comfort in spirituality.

Favorite Ways to Be Active

Aqua cycling, aqua Zumba,
modern dance, qigong, stand-up
paddle boarding, water skiing

Ailments and Injuries to Watch Out For

Athlete's foot, bunions and corns,
compulsive daydreaming, heel
spur, lethargy, sleep disorders

Scents and Essential Oils

Cassia, champaca, hibiscus, mango,
oakmoss, spruce, vetiver

Your Place
in the Stars

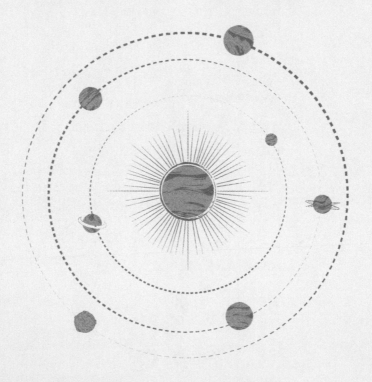

Sun Sign Yearbook

SUN SIGN	MOST LIKELY TO . . .	THE ZODIAC'S . . .
Aries	Be President	Bravest Sign
Taurus	Drape Themselves in Couture	Most Reliable Sign
Gemini	Turn Anything into a Celebration	Most Talkative Sign
Cancer	Give You a Hug	Most Considerate Sign
Leo	Win an Emmy, Grammy, Oscar, and Tony (EGOT)	Proudest Sign
Virgo	Save the Planet	Most Helpful Sign
Libra	Fight for Equity and Equality	Most Balanced Sign
Scorpio	Cast a Spell on You	Most Mysterious Sign
Sagittarius	Travel Around the World—Twice	Most Independent Sign
Capricorn	Bank Millions	Hardest-Working Sign
Aquarius	Colonize the Moon	Most Eccentric Sign
Pisces	Interpret Your Dreams	Most Sensitive Sign

Compatibility Matrix

Some signs just fit together; others are more likely to be at odds. But don't worry—you won't be enemies with every sign that doesn't align with yours. Similarly, just

	ARIES	TAURUS	GEMINI	CANCER	LEO
ARIES			♥	⚡	♥
TAURUS				♥	⚡
GEMINI	♥				♥
CANCER	⚡	♥			
LEO	♥	⚡	♥		
VIRGO		♥	⚡	♥	
LIBRA	⚡		♥	⚡	♥
SCORPIO		⚡		♥	⚡
SAGITTARIUS	♥		⚡		♥
CAPRICORN	⚡	♥		⚡	
AQUARIUS	♥	⚡	♥		⚡
PISCES		♥	⚡	♥	

because your signs match up doesn't mean you will always see eye-to-eye.

♥ =FRIEND, ⚡ =FOE

VIRGO	LIBRA	SCORPIO	SAGITTARIUS	CAPRICORN	AQUARIUS	PISCES
	⚡		♥	⚡	♥	
♥		⚡		♥	⚡	♥
⚡	♥		⚡		♥	⚡
♥	⚡	♥		⚡		♥
	♥	⚡	♥		⚡	
		♥	⚡	♥		⚡
			♥	⚡	♥	
♥				♥	⚡	♥
⚡	♥				♥	⚡
♥	⚡	♥				♥
	♥	⚡	♥			
⚡		♥	⚡	♥		

Famous Duos and Their Signs

These well-known pairs have relationships that were written in the stars—or were they? Turn to pages 168–169 to see how compatible different signs should or shouldn't be, then read on to understand more about the bonds between famous friends, colleagues, and paramours.

A$AP Rocky
LIBRA

+

Tyler, The Creator
PISCES

Beyoncé
VIRGO

+

Jay-Z
SAGITTARIUS

Emily Blunt
PISCES

+

John Krasinski
LIBRA

Anderson Cooper
GEMINI

+

Andy Cohen
GEMINI

Penélope Cruz
TAURUS

+

Javier Bardem
PISCES

Snoop Dogg
LIBRA

+

Martha Stewart
LEO

Tina Fey
TAURUS

+

Amy Poehler
VIRGO

Megan Fox
TAURUS

+

Machine Gun Kelly
TAURUS

Neil Patrick Harris
GEMINI

+

David Burtka
GEMINI

Prince Harry,
Duke of Sussex
VIRGO

+

Meghan Markle,
Duchess of Sussex
LEO

Taraji P. Henson
VIRGO

+

Mary J. Blige
CAPRICORN

King Princess
SAGITTARIUS

+

Quinn Wilson
ARIES

John Lennon
LIBRA

+

Paul McCartney
GEMINI

Jason Momoa
LEO

+

Lisa Bonet
SCORPIO

Barack Obama
LEO

+

Michelle Obama
CAPRICORN

Oprah
AQUARIUS

+

Gayle King
CAPRICORN

Sarah Paulson
SAGITTARIUS

+

Holland Taylor
CAPRICORN

Brad Pitt
SAGITTARIUS

+

George Clooney
TAURUS

Megan Rapinoe
CANCER

+

Sue Bird
LIBRA

Rihanna
PISCES

+

Cara Delevingne
LEO

Jada Pinkett Smith
VIRGO

+

Will Smith
LIBRA

Gwen Stefani
LIBRA

+

Blake Shelton
GEMINI

Sophie Turner
PISCES

+

Maisie Williams
ARIES

Sofía Vergara
CANCER

+

Joe Manganiello
CAPRICORN

Ali Wong
ARIES

+

Justin Hakuta
LIBRA

Perfect Careers for Each Sign

Some signs are predisposed to be doctors or day traders, while other signs make great coaches or broadcast journalists. Read on to discover which jobs and industries might be ideal for you.

Aries

Overflowing with self-confidence and courage, Aries flourishes in business, entertainment, finance, government, medicine, the military, public relations, and sales. But, as born leaders, Aries can motivate and inspire just about any team.

Taurus

Ruled by Venus, goddess of beauty and abundance, Taurus does well in architecture, banking, entertainment, and fashion. An excellent sense of taste coupled with a desire to acquire makes Taurus a talented museum curator, gallerist, or interior designer.

Gemini

Geminis are terrific talkers, so they excel in careers that let them communicate and interact with others, such as administration, advertising, communications, education, event planning, human resources, the law, marketing, media, and sales.

Cancer

As natural caretakers, Cancers thrive in all careers because they always work hard in order to provide for their loved ones. Their characteristic empathy especially lends itself to childcare, early education, food service and hospitality, health care and medicine, and real estate.

Leo

Mix a love of the spotlight with an opinionated streak and willingness to break the rules, and you have the recipe for Leo's best career: heading up a visionary start-up. Prosperous Leos can also be found in apparel and jewelry, business, entertainment, and finance.

Virgo

Virgo sees what's wrong in the world and wants to fix it, so this sign finds purpose in environmental activism and social justice. The Virgo talent for organizing information lends itself to fulfilling careers in data management, library science, and all kinds of research, too.

Libra

With a pronounced sense of fairness and equality, Libras make amazing lawyers. But their people skills and willingness to follow the rules definitely work well in diplomacy and government, mediation, public relations, and sports.

Scorpio

Scorpio's secrecy, aura of mystery, and deep-seated need for privacy are ideal characteristics for a life of espionage. But Scorpios also shine in careers related to archaeology, criminal justice, investigative journalism, psychology, and science.

Sagittarius

Free-spirited Sagittarius loves to travel, so any career in the travel industry—from being a flight attendant to leading tours—is an excellent fit. In addition, this sign loves sharing knowledge. As such, academia, personal coaching, publishing, and religion are full of Sagittariuses.

Capricorn

Capricorns care about the past, especially its traditions, making them brilliant anthropologists, archivists, curators, and historians. Regardless of which path they choose, however, Capricorns' tremendous work ethic will help them get ahead. They may even work multiple jobs at once.

Aquarius

Aquariuses are the inventors of the zodiac, constantly experimenting, often with an eye toward helping humanity. This future-oriented sign relishes working in aerospace and technology, engineering, philanthropy, politics, science, social work, and web design.

Pisces

Pisces succeed in jobs that require creative thinking, from arts, entertainment, and media to less obvious choices like entrepreneurialism, finance, and project management. With their almost bottomless wells of compassion, this sign blooms in health care, medicine, and psychology as well.

About the Author

Jessica Allen read her first horoscope at age nine. Since then, she has written for the *Boston Globe*, CNN, the *Independent*, *McSweeney's*, *Mental Floss*, *The Onion's A.V. Club*, the *Washington Post*, *Writer's Digest*, and many other publications. A Scorpio based in New York, she's married to a Virgo, and together they're raising a Taurus.